HOW TO GET MONEY

THE MASTER KEY TO SUCCESS & WEALTH

by David Jambrovic

Legal Disclaimer

Table of Contents

Chapter One:
Introduction

You Already Know

Getting money is one of the easiest things to do. And we are doing it all the time.

You have this book in your hands, don't you? Well, in order to do that, there had to be money first—even if it wasn't necessarily your money. Perhaps this book was a gift or someone simply handed it to you but money was used by someone to buy it. Even if you are reading this in a library, you most likely needed some gas money or transportation ticket to go here. The library also needs money to pay their bills and employees, amongst other things. Money underlies virtually everything we do. So much of human behavior, from grand events like enjoyable trips to the cup of coffee you enjoy in the morning, involves the exchange of money.

So you already know how to get money. The purpose of this book is to motivate and to inspire you to figure out how to get more of it. You need enough money to live the lifestyle that you desire, to have whatever you want, whenever you want, however you want, and on your terms. That is the craft that some people have mastered. They managed to make money come to them, instead of chasing after it. They even give it away to charities, foundations, hospitals, universities, libraries, and all sorts of causes of their choice. What did they do differently? They don't just earn money, they create money but money doesn't simply come to them. There's much more to it than that. They don't go looking for money but rather to provide value and that is how they create it. Now, how do you do that and what is the difference between earning and creating money? You do that by paying a stiff price for it. It's kind of like paying a ticket to Disneyland. Once you can afford it, you get your ticket and you enter. If you try to cheat and sneak in, you are soon exposed and are kicked out quickly. Think of people who made monetary gains rapidly and not by their own effort, then lost it all. Or people who did it unethically. They did not pay the price for that ticket, they snacked. The difference between earning money and creating money is that you will always only get enough for basic living. When you create money, you create for others the chance for them to gain their own money or other benefits in one form or another. Thus, you reap multiple rewards and money comes after you. Let me give you an example.

A couple of years ago, I met Marko, a particularly wealthy gentleman from Montenegro, and I was curious as to how he made his fortune. In the 1980's, the economy of Montenegro wasn't in the best state. On top of everything, he had a mother who needed medical care and that was just too much of a strain on Marko's budget. He was in his early twenties and, like many young people, could not find a job to support himself there. On the other hand, western Europe was booming, so Marko decided to take a trip to search for a job in Germany. He really did not like to leave his home, but he accepted the fact that this was the price he needed to pay in order to secure medications for his mother. He knocked on his best friend Luka's door and asked him: "Are you in?". Luka said "Yes", and the next morning they were on their way to western Germany. Soon enough, they were hired as construction workers to build houses. Associating with the German workers, Marko picked up the German language quickly. The German workers had more experience as they had been on the site for a longer time. They were disciplined and displayed a fantastic work ethic. Marko paid attention to their skills and began implementing them himself. Marko, inspired by skilled workers, improved his habits and was always putting in extra effort even though he wasn't being paid extra. He changed the way that he was viewing his job. He saw blessings that enabled him to take care of his mother. He had faith and discipline, thanks to paying attention to the right things. On the other hand, his friend Luka was discontent, always complaining, asking Marko why he was being so stupid, saying that they should work as little as possible since they were being paid anyway. This characteristic of Marko did not go unnoticed by his bosses. So, they promoted him to foreman as they were very pleased with his initiative. Luka, on the other hand, changed his job for a better paid one. He became a waiter. Luka soon lost his job as the restaurant needed to reduce their workforce in order to save money. One day, Marco's bosses asked him if he could bring them any other skilled people for work. "Sure", he said, and he brought them a few other people from Montenegro with great work ethics. Now, Marko was paid a percentage from each person he brought to the company whenever they received their paycheck because he brought more people into the business. He was paid so much money that he decided to open a business of his own and employed more people there. He opened an agency that was finding people construction jobs and he provided construction companies with a great workforce. That was his start to creating wealth for himself.

Through his dedication to the work, Marco was able to earn money not just for himself but he also created opportunities in the form of jobs for others and at the same time attracted more good workers for the construction company. He helped the people he brought into the company to make their money and he helped out company owners to get more and better work done so they got their money too because the houses were built at a faster pace.

Marco took the following steps:

1. He made a decision—to find a job for himself.

2. He accepted the price for it, to move abroad.

3. He took action by taking a trip to Germany.

4. He paid attention to his job and his employer's needs.

5. He shifted his associations by hanging out with German employees and more skilled workers.

6. He shifted his working habits and provided more service than he was paid for.

7. He shifted his thoughts and was grateful for the opportunities.

8. He had faith as he was performing his job with excellence.

9. He was disciplined and a good worker.

10. He contributed to the company by bringing in more workers.

11. He was creative and came up with idea of opening an agency making it easier to find a suitable working force and provide jobs to others.

12. All along, he was using the Master Key, the key that will be reviled in this book.

Getting money was the easiest thing for Marco at that point in his life. It was just pouring in. The money was attracted to him.

Now let me tell you the secret, dear reader. You have all the power. You have the ability (and the responsibility) to make a decision and to stick to it. You are the one who will have to commit. I can only give you words that will evolve into ideas, ideas that will evolve into inspiration. You don't need to look around for anyone else's approval. You have to approve yourself! You don't need to look around for the situation to change. Start now, wherever you are and with whatever you have at this moment. The only thing you have is *now*. That's it. The past is gone and the future is full of uncertainty. You cannot choose your circumstances, but you can choose your response to them. Just as the captain of a boat going down the river cannot straighten out the curves of the bank, he can adjust its course by controlling the helm.

There are literally millions of ways to become a millionaire and you can certainly find yours. And it's almost impossible for you not to achieve it if you are really serious about it.

This book provides a roadmap to help you navigate, but *you* are the one who has to do the work, *on yourself*, to become a better, more honest version of you. Because the best thing you can do is to become more of yourself. The Creator made you perfect, so the more of your true self you give to the world, the more successful and happier you become. You are the original. You are here to give yourself to the world. You are a gift to this world, you are a present to humanity. It's time to unwrap yourself. You are the only one who knows your answers. Each one of us is a unique human being and each one of us has our own truth, our own answers.

Ultimately, this book can inform and inspire you, but only *you* can help *you*. Arm yourself with knowledge, but know that real action depends on *your* initiative and discipline. Seminars, workshops, and books are just tools. You are the craftsman, the artist, the meister. You are the king, and now is the time to claim your kingdom.

The Success Pyramid

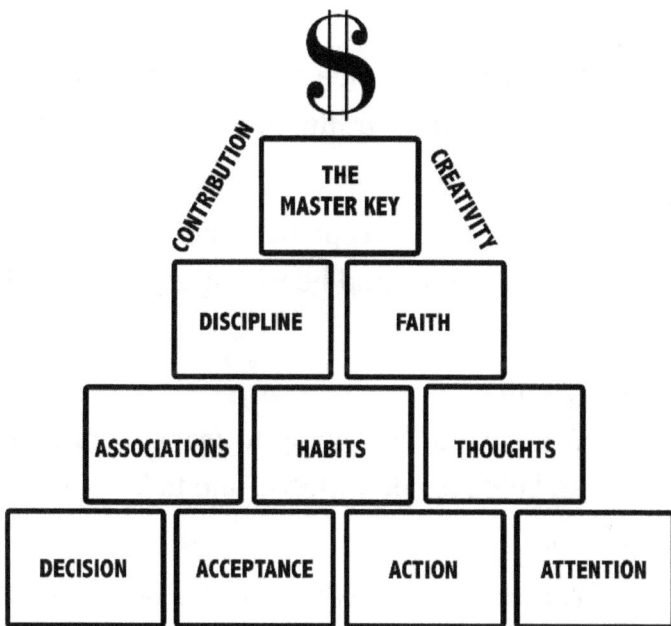

What Are You Getting?

This book is the result of over a decade of research that I did in order to discover how to get money. It will bring you a roadmap and the Master Key to success.

The roadmap is in the shape of a pyramid and it begins with the first floor:

1. Decision

   You have to decide that you want to change things in your life, your results, yourself.

2. Acceptance

   You have to accept that there is a price for everything and be willing to pay the asking price.

3. Action

   You have to be willing to feel comfortable, to being uncomfortable, and to keep moving.

4. Attention

   You have to be willing to be open and alert enough to recognize opportunities.

That brings us to the second floor of our pyramid where you will have to shift your:

5. Associations
   Your results are correlated directly with your surroundings, things, and people around you.

6. Habits
   Your habits are your inner programming that always brings you to the same results. Now, you want these results to be ones that you would like to have.

7. Thoughts
   Who possesses your mind? To what and to whom are you paying your attention? Note the word "paying".

The third floor of the pyramid contains two ingredients that are carried out through the Master Key.

8. Discipline
   You have to excel in something and practice it through discipline. You have to be organized.

9. Faith
   You have to believe and to see yourself already achieving your goal.

And that brings us to the fourth floor where the Master Key resides.

10. The Master Key

   This is the key through which all sustainable success is achieved. To use the key properly, you have to pass two guards:

   Guard No. 1: Contribution
   You have to find out how you can serve.

   Guard No. 2: Creativity

   You have to figure out what you can create.

   To get an appointment with the two guards that hold the Master Key, you have to isolate yourself and delve deep into yourself. Then you wait for the invitation. When you get the invitation, it sets your password for the two guards that let you use the Master Key.

How Is Money Being Attracted

To attract money, it's not so much about what you *do* as *who you are,* because who you are dictates how you do it. You can do virtually anything you want, master it, and reap the rewards. I used to say that even if you do the simplest thing in the world such as stacking one pebble on top of another and you become great at it, you can reap rewards from it and be compensated handsomely.

Sure enough, one day I visited Sausalito, a small town by the bay just across from San Francisco on the other side of the Golden Gate Bridge. I was walking by the shore and saw a crowd surrounding a chap. The guy would line up about a dozen pebbles from the beach in a way that they looked like an incredible statue defying gravity. It was just amazing and appeared very unnatural. He charged $100 and up for each sculpture and all he would do was pack the pebbles in a plastic bag and provide a sketch showing how to reassemble them. What was his secret? He mastered a craft, an art form that people hadn't seen before, and they wanted it.

People don't get paid based on what they would like to be paid, but for what value they give as a person and for what they have to offer to the world. Money is something that you attract based on the person you are. If people know that you are a great investor and know how and where to invest, wouldn't people rush to you to handle their money?

There is a big difference between reaching after something and becoming (being) someone. Virtually everybody can hold something for a second, but to keep it, you have to be it. A valley person can drive a Bentley, Ferrari, or a Lamborghini for a minute, but to get it, they have to figure out how to become even more valuable to society. You can't just invest, you have to become an investor. You don't just *reach* your goal; you have to *become* your goal. Each one of us is on their own path—to get to their own destination to become great at something. And this world needs people of excellence, masters of their craft, people who deliver!

Two people can start the same business at the same time, make the same investment, enjoy the same opportunities—yet end up with completely opposite results. It's not merely the business that matters, it's the person running it. While other factors may dictate success or failure, it primarily comes down to the individual leading it.

You get more money by *being* more, not by *doing* more. By being more, doing more will take care of itself.

This is essentially what happens when you learn a new skill. Many people who are good at one thing also can excel in related fields. For example, singers often transition to acting. A person who is a proficient stock trader will likely succeed in other forms of trading. Once someone masters their ability in one area, they often can apply those same principles and qualities in another field. If you learn how to drive a sedan, you will know how to drive a convertible. If you know how to drive a convertible, just make a small adjustment and you will figure out how to drive a truck. Once you learn how to play a guitar, it's easier to learn how to play a piano or cello or almost any other instrument. You already have the advantage of understanding how music works and the essence of harmonies and tones. Once you master how to navigate, switching does not require you to start from scratch, just to make some minor adjustments. When you learn how to drive one vehicle, switching to another requires some adjustment instead of starting to learn all over again. You are already a driver. Once you master how to get money, it's just like changing vehicles which you already know how to operate. You become rich.

This book is here to inspire you, so you can figure out and determine for yourself what kind of person you should become mentally, emotionally, and character-wise to attract what you want. The person you are—your habits, character, mindset, and emotions—has already brought you this far so there is every reason to expect a successful outcome. Now it's all about honing these abilities to work most effectively for you.

Chapter Two:
Decision

Growth Starts From Discomfort

Probably you've heard the saying—often attributed to Albert Einstein—that "The definition of insanity is doing the same thing over and over again but expecting different results." Like they say, "Old ways won't open new doors". While doing something repeatedly might help you develop a particular skill, that skill will be much more useful if you can figure out how to improve it as time goes by. That's how leaps of success happen.

Do you know how to drive a car? Do you remember your experience *before* you knew which pedal was which and how it all works? At first, driving is uncomfortable; you have to think consciously about every little move you make. Then after some time, it becomes natural and automatic. And it's vastly quicker and more efficient than walking, which is what you were doing before. Going from walking to driving is quite a leap. In fact, when the first cars came out, many people were scared by these new "machines". Then they realized how cars could make their lives much more efficient.

The same thing applies to making major progress in life. In order to grow, we must go for it. We must overcome the fear of discomfort. We have to act despite the fear. We must step out of our comfort zone in order to grow. We have to learn to be comfortable with feeling uncomfortable. We have to do it consciously at first; then, after we do it for a long enough period of time, it becomes more "automatic".

Yet even over a long period, most people don't progress financially. They end up with exactly the same amount for most of their lives—and that's because they keep doing the same things over and over again. They are afraid to learn how to drive and thereby overcome traveling huge distances because it feels safer just to walk. But is walking really safer than driving? Is driving really safer than flying? Last time I checked, statistics show that flying is much safer than driving.

HOW TO GET MONEY

The only way to change your income is to change yourself—including your thinking, approach, beliefs, and methods. This might be just a minor shift for some people; for others, it requires a complete transformation. Sometimes, you have to reinvent yourself totally to achieve the change you seek.

But how does one *change* themself in such a significant way? One method is to pay attention to the ways of someone who already achieved what you would like to achieve. I have a rule—to take advice from people who are already doing what I would like to do. I listen to advice about relationships or marriage only from people who have spent at least ten good years in a marriage themselves. I take financial advice from those who are in a better financial standing than I. You wouldn't take advice on how to get a muscular six-pack from a person with a flabby "spare tire".

Strangely enough, people who are eager to offer you advice about relationships are often the ones without a history of successful relationships—and those with perpetual money problems are quick to dispense wisdom about finances. Would you listen to someone who *studied* skydiving in a classroom, yet never stepped out of a plane, or from someone who is skydiving on a regular basis? Again, you want to hear from people who already have attained results that you would like to achieve, whatever the endeavor. Free advice is, in the end, often the most expensive kind and it usually involves a hidden cost down the road.

Some people invest a lot of time and resources to become an expert on a subject or to perfect a skill. *Those* are the people from whom you want to solicit advice. And if you have to pay up front for the advice, it is probably good—likely even expert—advice. If a person puts some money and time into developing a skill or a trade, they value it, and charge for it.

If you are the fastest paddler in your boat, it's time to find yourself another boat with a crew that is helping you to speed up rather than dragging you back. A lot of people feel comfortable telling others what they should do when they haven't yet been there themselves.

When it comes to money, formulate your own goal, but you can *copy rich people's methods of doing things*. Emulate the behaviors and patterns of wealthy and successful individuals and adapt them to your own life and business. Wealthy people are wealthy because they do certain things in certain ways. It's not good to try to compete with them, nor envy them. It's better to be inspired by them, and build your own collage of your character. Not everything they do will necessarily work for you—but applying their methods is a good first step.

A friend of mine was in a barber shop the other day and while having his haircut, he struck up a conversation with the barber. The barber was complaining that he needs a new car. Funny enough, my friend wanted to get rid of a fairly new Jaguar for only $3,000 because he has quite a few cars and this one was just for business use so he no longer needed it. Considering the age and condition of the car, that was an amazing deal and the barber could easily afford to pay that much. However, the barber said that he wants a convertible Ford Mustang so he'll pass on the opportunity. Well, the same age of used Jaguar was over four times more expensive at best at any dealership. The barber had big dreams and wanted a muscle car, yet he passed up the opportunity so easily. Even if he bought it and immediately resold it, he could easily make a few thousand dollars. And he could use that for a down payment on his dream car. But it just wasn't good enough for him. Average people usually don't amount to anything because they can't make good decisions. Nothing is ever good enough; they always think there's something better out there—and out of their reach. It feels more comfortable to sit back and have nothing than to struggle in pursuit of a goal or to venture outside one's comfort zone. As soon you put yourself out there, there's a risk that people will judge you—that people might not like you. It's safer to do nothing, to be nothing, and to blame others. "Rich people? They just got lucky," some might say. But did they really? Often, they didn't; they put themselves out there, they take risks, and they take responsibility for their destiny by placing it in their own hands. They *possess their own lives*. Not their neighbors, not their friends, not their circumstances determine who they are. They run their own lives and create their own economy, their own future and their own fortune.

If things have not worked out well for you so far, you can always change your approach and figure out how to do things differently. If what you've been doing works for you—and you're already thriving financially—you might discover some ideas about how to grow even bigger. After all, nothing is static—and nothing is guaranteed! Any sense of security is often just an illusion. You must keep reinventing yourself because the "you" that made you $100,000 is not the same person who will get you $1,000,000. You have to make and remake yourself. You have to upgrade yourself first in order to upgrade your income. A celebrity movie star gets paid way more to do a TV commercial than an unknown actor does. A financial expert gets paid more than a financial adviser. You have to *be* more to *get* more. The best investments that I ever made were not financial nor in real estate. The most valuable investments I made were investments in myself—in my knowledge, in my skills, and in my quality of life.

It's often said that half of global wealth is held by 1% of the world's population. And I am pretty sure that if you would distribute that money from each of these people, they would find a way to get it back—because money is a tangible asset that they receive *because of their energy* and the service they provide. Our singular goal should not merely be to copy the business models of rich people, but rather to emulate how wealthy people act and spread their energy. Consider studying how they treat others, how they carry themselves, how they disperse their wealth, which non-profits they support, and perhaps most importantly, what they plan to do next—not just what they are doing in this moment.

Remember: it is energy, not money, which determines whether one will ascend to great heights in this world. The more energy we have, the more we can endeavor to achieve. And that is how we should copy the rich: in energy *expended*, not money *expected*.

Two Kinds Of People

There are basically two kinds of people in this world: Achievers and Deceivers. Achievers work all the time while Deceivers work only when everybody is watching, people who work on their development by creating and serving, and people who think they can manipulate their way in. Libraries and bookstores are full of books for the second kind—teaching them how to use deception, to put others down, to manipulate or to control people. The truth is that all these unscrupulous manipulations might work for a day or two, but in the long run, they never do. Most of those so-called "gurus" have no clue what they are talking about. How can you teach women how to seduce, to really manipulate a man, if you are a single old gal with no meaningful relationship and a number of previous divorces? They should teach them good values and principals, because those are required for a sustainable marriage. Kissing all the frogs will keep you busy from finding your prince.

The difference is that achievers progress slowly in the beginning because doing things the right way might take a bit longer. People who are doing things in this way are the ten percent who have their lives figured out. People in the second group, the deceivers, appear to be progressing rapidly; but in reality, they are spinning in circles and going nowhere. In other words, as old and used as it sounds, "Players always get played in the end".

If you are playing to win, you have to play by the rules—obeying high moral standards, obeying the law, and giving respect. That is the only way. Everything else is just an illusion, an illusion of success which is always just short-term success.

It's not money that will make you valuable somehow; rather, it's your inherent value that will create wealth. And in order to be valuable, you have to determine your values. The principles you live by determine your destiny—so what are your values?

Your income is proportional to the value you provide to the job market. While imagination can be a good motor to get you going, you have to master a discipline first.

You know that feeling when you start seeing someone and at the beginning, that person agrees on everything you say, but as time passes by, their actions tell a completely different story? Wealthy and successful people are able to evaluate people quickly in most instances. The people being deceived almost always know the truth, they just decide to ignore it because they want so strongly to believe in that lie. Even when it sounds so unbelievable! If you listen carefully to any person, you will hear what that person really is saying. People always know when they are being played (or lied to), yet they refuse to recognize it and take action. It often is said that everyone is a teacher if you know how to listen. But more than that, everybody will tell you who they are if you pay attention to what are they really saying. Pay attention to the red flags. That is why successful people are quick with their decisions. When my friend, the previously mentioned multi-millionaire who had one of his first big job offers, showed up to the meeting a couple of minutes late, he lost that job that day. The rich value their time, and if you don't show respect for their time, they take that personally. From then on, he was always on time. In the language of successful people, "on time" means fifteen minutes early. If you arrive on time—you are late and if you are late—don't even bother to show up. You see, success has its rules and they are universal no matter the country, culture, or language, no matter if it was hundreds or thousands of years ago. If you are serious about money, you better act like money.

HOW TO GET MONEY

Chapter Three:

Acceptance

What Are You Willing To Give?

Are you willing to give what it takes to get what you want?

One beautiful September afternoon in Scottsdale, Arizona, I had just finished attending a three-day seminar and was waiting outside the hotel for the limousine to pick me up and take me to PHX airport. The limo arrived promptly and I hopped in. I exchanged pleasantries with the driver, who told me his name was Tom, and as the journey started, we talked casually about various subjects. The driver had an interesting story to tell about none other than himself.

Earlier that day, Tom received a phone call from one of his colleagues, another limousine driver named Jim. Jim had picked up a popular celebrity from the airport and the celebrity had a somewhat strange request. There was a game at the stadium that day and he needed badly to be there. He then promised to pay Jim the sum of $1000 if he would help him get inside the stadium without being stopped at any of the security checkpoints on the way. Jim was bewildered and did not know what to do or say, so he called Tom for advice. Tom, on the other hand, saw his opportunity and told Jim that he would take $100 out of the $1000 Jim would be paid if he told him what to do. Jim agreed to this deal and Tom gave his advice.

He told Jim to drive down to the stadium and give each security guard at every checkpoint $100 and then tell them the name of the celebrity he had in the car. Doing this would enable him to pass through freely and deliver the celebrity to his desired destination. There were only three checkpoints so he would only have to pay $300. Jim got angry and yelled at Tom that he was crazy to think he would just give out the money he had earned like that. Tom then replied, "It's up to you if you want to invest and get a high return or not. I would surely do that if I were in your shoes. Remember, you still owe me $100 for the advice I just gave you." Though Jim got great advice from Tom, he still had a hard time listening to it. He would have had to spend $400 to garner a $600 profit, but he balked at the idea. Spending a relatively small amount of money in order to get more money was unreasonable to him.

In order to get what you want, you have to pay the asking price, not merely what are you willing to give. Because it's not about how much it costs, but how much is the return.

What Is Money?

Money can be both simple and complex. The basic concept is familiar to anyone; yet the definitions and meaning can be different to almost *everyone*. To me, money is just an idea, or a form of *energy*. The more you have, the more you can share, help, do, and enjoy. Therefore, money is a tool that can help us improve our lives and support others.

Money is also a *currency*—something that has a certain amount of value and can be exchanged for something that we need and/or desire. The term "currency" usually refers to money, but it can mean almost anything of value. It's a medium of exchange. Your word can be your currency if you are a person of integrity.

I came to the conclusion that two major factors define the value of a currency: trustworthiness plus the size and health of the economy. For example, a certain country's value of money is determined by that country's stability and trust. If a dishonest government that prints more money every time they are in need runs that country, then their money devaluates. But if a government is trustworthy and their economy is in good standing, then its money has guaranteed value. The same is true for people. If a person has integrity and something valuable to offer, that person is highly respected.

I consider my most valuable currency to be my time and my emotions. Therefore, I expend these only on things that can benefit me in some way. You can always get more money, but you don't have any more time on this planet than what you're allotted—and none of us truly knows how much we have left. So I am selective about what I get involved in emotionally and physically. I prefer to engage in activities that I consider to meet my standards for value.

Saying money can't bring you happiness is like saying a car can't bring you anywhere just because you don't know how to drive one. Yes in order to have more money, you have to be trained in how to get more money. You're lucky if you can find yourself a mentor, a coach who can line it up for you. But if you can't, you have to do it yourself. It's the same way people have to learn how to fly an airplane, how to use a computer and the majority of complex things for the first time. Once you know how, you always know how.

Once you learn how to play an instrument, you will always know how to play it. The fact is that people need to be trained in how to deal with money as well. And the only training that most people have is by people who raised them, the school system, and places were they grew up. We love and cherish them for it, but depending on their own financial training, what had they actually transferred to us? How to get money or how to get rid of money? People with wealthier parents most likely had a better education or training. But a person who comes from a different background needs to untrain themself and learn how to get money.

How much money you can get is in direct correlation with your subconscious programming. It's your pre-set set of values, mindset, and character. We all have been pre-set or programmed with our beliefs as to what is our high ceiling regarding money. And that is how much is going to come to each one of us. Unless . . . . Yes, we can reprogram ourselves. We can re-set. This book works with ideas explaining how it all works and what tools we can use in order to do that. You can get all the right opportunities in your life, but if you are not ready to accept them, it's not going to work for you.

Now meet Tara. Tara was a typical woman who moved to Hollywood to pursue a movie career. There she met her boyfriend, Greg. One day, one of their friends advised them to join a church that was known to be attended by many big movie producers. Tara did not see much value in practicing to be an actor but believed that connections alone and her stunning looks were going to bring her an acting career. So finally one day, she was given an opportunity for a role in a TV commercial. She came to the set totally unprepared and her boyfriend Greg did not help the situation as he was blaming her for her failure to prepare. Tara and Greg ended up in a big fight on the set and were kicked out of the studio. They blamed everything else but themselves. The truth of the matter is that they were lacking self-discipline, manners, and professionalism. So, no matter what kind of chances some people get in life, they will always find a way to get out of it and of course, they will always blame it on circumstances and other people.

Now meet Angie. Angie had a job interview to work for a car tire manufacturer and she claimed in her application that she speaks four languages— English, Portuguese, Spanish, and French. The truth was that she could barely speak a few words of

French, let alone the other languages. Actually, her best friend advised her to make that claim anyway, and that it wouldn't really matter, that it would give her an advantage over the other candidates. As it turned out, she was the most qualified applicant and she was hired. Soon after, the CEO of the company she worked for had to take a trip to Europe to negotiate some deals overseas. He took Angie along as he needed a translator. They visited Spain, Portugal, England, and Switzerland. After they returned home, the company started mass production of tires. But they needed to buy the raw rubber materials first. However, they ordered way too much. They only needed a little to ramp up the production for the new markets they just gained but didn't realize it initially. Finally, they shipped their products to the European countries which gave them contracts. However, soon after, their shipment to Switzerland was returned because the wrong type of tires were shipped. You see, Angie completely misunderstood the Swiss gentleman because her French was insufficient and caused the whole mess. Not surprisingly, she was fired immediately. However, fast forward—Angie took this life lesson seriously and she went back to study. Today, she speaks six languages fluently and she owns her own company.

You see that happen when people demand rewards before they are ready to receive them.

What Is Currency?

The strict definition of currency is a generally accepted type of money which is issued by a government and circulated within an economy. It is also used as a medium of exchange for goods and services, and includes coins and paper notes. Each country has its own currency. While currencies are usually specific to a country, some countries accept other currencies as legal tender. Examples include the Euro, Yen, and US Dollar, for instance.

As long as you are willing to pay the asking price for it, you can have almost everything in life. But before considering the price, you have to determine the type of currency that you need in order to complete a specific goal. For example, you reside in the U.S. and you want to treat yourself to a delicious meal in a fancy restaurant. The price of this meal is 35 dollars; but you only have 35 Japanese yen in your pocket. In the world market today, the exchange rate of yen to dollars is about one dollar for 100 yen. You therefore have just 35 cents with you so you cannot afford the meal.

Because currencies differ, you need to know the purchasing power of a given currency in relation to the product or service you want to purchase. If you only have a GED (high school diploma), chances are next to zero that you'll be accepted as a lawyer to a law firm. That's the power of education.

A common misconception is that the busier a person is, the more wealth they will be able to acquire. But most of the time, this is not the case. If it were, then every manual laborer would be unimaginably rich. There is a widely held yet usually false belief that struggle is evidence that you are achieving something. But activity is not the same as productivity. You must determine what *type* of work to do and how to carry it out most efficiently to get the results you want. In order to become more successful, you need to develop a craft or skill in high demand. If your skill is not in high demand, your reward (pay) will be low. If you keep developing your skills, so will your reward (pay) grow.

It's a similar dynamic as in a relationship. One partner has to have a trait that attracts the other, and vice versa. For example, perhaps you are interested in a socialite—someone who likely would be interested in you if you are presentable, relatively good-looking, educated, and have good manners. It is only when you possess these qualities that it is possible for you to have a relationship with that type of person—because you're interested in the same kinds of things and you both complement each other's traits. A well-dressed, educated, mature woman does not want to date boys. She needs an equally qualified man. It just would not work otherwise.

Too many people see other people succeed at something and they think they can just copy their methods and enjoy the same success. The problem with this approach is that it ignores a critical component—the *qualities* that made those people successful.

Marketable qualities serve as the "currency" that you need to have in order to get what you want. The maxim that "Nothing valuable comes free" should be at the back of your mind all the time. Even if you think you've gained something for free, there is a delayed payment that will arrive at your doorstep with interest calculated.

Some individuals simply aren't willing to give what it takes. Average people are looking for ways to escape reality by minding other people's business, seeking constant entertainment. Successful people are looking for ways how to reshape reality to match their vision. And they are willing to pay the asking price for it.

Thinking of Time As Currency

Not only is time our most valuable currency; it's actually the only *real* currency we have. After all, we theoretically can acquire money in limitless quantities—but there is no way to get more time. So having a day job is basically exchanging your time for money. And generally, you can have only one job—at the most, two or three. There is always a limit on how much time you can exchange directly for money, since a day has only twenty-four hours.

But what if you had a business and other people worked *for* you? This would afford you more time to create another enterprise . . . and possibly another one, and . . . A "job" will monopolize your time and keep you running like a hamster on a hamster wheel. One way to change this is to think bigger. After all, while you are looking to buy a condo, another person is looking to buy the entire building.

Working for wages is a start, but it is *not* the best way to make money because you're just exchanging your time for money, your energy for another form of energy in fact. Remember: I see money as a form of energy. But if you can pay more and do less in exchange, you actually find a way to *receive* time. That is how the most successful people in the world "buy" more time: by spending money on meaningful and time-saving measures like outsourcing and delegating. They hire other people to do little and time consuming things, like cleaning or repairing things. They hire experts to get their opinions, rather than wasting their time with research. They then use the time they receive in much more productive ways. On the other hand, some people are trying to do everything by themselves. A person of excellence knows what jobs to take and what to delegate. It's an investment that can pay vast dividends. The more time you have, the more money you can make.

Some people think that starting a business will make them rich automatically. A business can be lucrative, but it's a time-consuming venture. If your business requires your constant presence, then it's actually a *job*, not just a business. It's important to delegate as much work as possible to other people. Do you think Bill Gates and Steve Jobs sat in the factory and assembled the computers? Do you think they actually created all of the algorithms that made their machines function, or obsessed over the design? Even Jobs, who had a reputation for being a hands-on control freak, was forced to yield some control—a move that worked well both for him and for Apple.

Business leaders who thrive manage to part with some of their energy (money) to get a substantial amount of energy (time) back in return. They are then able to use that newly gifted time to create and to innovate further. In turn, they can hire better leaders and more intelligent team members to whom to delegate tasks. Subsequently, those team leaders can hire a team of *their* own, delegating some of their energy in exchange for an abundance of time. At each of these levels, time multiplies opportunity, increasing success across the board.

Let's say you own a restaurant. If you need to be there all the time, you're left with no time to grow. And if you're not growing, you're moving backwards, not forwards—because in the end, nothing actually stands still. Maybe you don't notice it right away, but when you become aware of it, it's usually too late.

As the owner, you shouldn't be mired in menial tasks. The restaurant desperately needs you to find creative ways to balance expenses, develop innovative new menu options, and build a strong marketing platform to attract customers.

Ideally, you would like as much free time as possible for yourself after you put your business on a strong footing. Then you can expand to build another restaurant, a chain of restaurants, or even a franchise. Once you multiply your energy, you can multiply your team exponentially, greatly enlarging your earning potential. At that point, you don't even need to be confined to one *type* of business, and you can expand into other industries.

The other day, I went to my Accountant/CPA to handle some regular accounting business. We had a little conversation and he told me a story about this doctor who would do everything himself and he always wondered how at the end of the day he wasn't making as much money as he originally anticipated when he started his private practice. And when I say he was doing everything by himself, I mean everything, from cleaning the instruments to cleaning the floors and bathrooms at the end of the each business day. The accountant told the doctor that if you want to make more money, you have to delegate some of the work and pay other people to do it for you, so you can make your money doing what you do best. Just compare how much a medical specialist is paid per hour compared to an assistant who would clean the instruments, or better yet, someone who would just be paid to clean the floors and bathrooms. Ever since then, the doctor's financial situation went through the roof because he used his time wisely. The next door office was just offered to lease so he leased it and joined the practices so he could see more patients and get paid more at the same time.

When you free up your time, your mind becomes fertile ground for new ideas and you can focus on creative growth and opportunity. For instance—I didn't always want to write a book. But as I learned throughout my own journey—and as I received more time—I had more time to fill. And I realized I could offer readers my own energy, in book form, to help others exponentially. After the initial investment of time in writing it, its benefit to others is theoretically infinite. It doesn't take any more time for me to help 100, 10,000, or even 10,000,000 people with this book since the energy has been expended and the Universe has welcomed it. Just think, if you could delegate some of your work to others and free some more time for yourself, what goods could you create for this world? What ideas that are hiding inside you would come to light to serve humanity?

Chapter Four:
Attention

Godard And His Nine Sons

Once upon a time, there was a wise man named Godard who had nine sons. The time eventually came for his sons to leave home and build houses of their own. But Godard had only three cows that he could pass on to his sons, so he had to decide which three sons would get the cows.

So Godard took his nine sons to a nearby lake. He had three boats ready; in each boat would be three sons. However, there were no paddles, so they had to use their hands to paddle to the other side of the lake where there were three cows waiting for the sons who came first with their boat dry. The sons were a little surprised that they had to keep their boat dry; nevertheless, they got ready and started off.

When they reached the middle of the lake, all nine sons realized that all three boats had leaks and that water was pouring in. The three sons in the first boat ignored the leakage altogether and continued to paddle with their hands at a faster pace. Soon enough, their boat sank and they had to swim back to shore.

The three sons in the second boat saw what happened to the first one so they invested all their energy into keeping all the water outside of the boat. Only when all the water was out would they paddle and advance a little, then go back to removing the water with their hands.

The sons in the third boat organized themselves so that the son with the longest hands was only paddling, the shortest one's task was to keep bailing out water, and the middle son sat in between. When there was too much water inside, he helped remove it; when there was just a little, he helped with the paddling. Most of the time, he was paddling.

In the meantime, the three sons in the second boat became so tired that they had to give up. They advanced too slowly and too little. Finally, the third boat reached the shore, and the three sons in the third boat picked up the boat, turned it over, and poured out all the water left in it. Their father gave them the three cows.

The moral of this story is this: where do you concentrate your energy, where is your focus? On paying bills and cutting expenses—or on making more money? You cannot just disregard your dues like the first three sons did, but you can't focus *solely* on cutting expenses. You have to figure out how to get ahead while spending enough to keep your venture afloat and eliminating only what's necessary to move forward. And once you reach the land on the other side, things become as easy as turning over the boat to empty out the water.

The key is to feel good about paying your bills and to be grateful that you have enough, so you don't waste your time or energy on it. Then, you can focus on ways to get *more* money.

Shift Your Focus

Many people dream about having a million dollars. But does their inner talk indicate that they're ready to receive it? What do they keep telling themselves? They often spend time justifying why they *still don't have* what they desire.

There is no bad or good in nature; it just *is*. *We* assign meaning to the events that occur in our lives. *We* decide if something that happened in our past was bad or good. It's up to us to define it. And that is exactly the thing that makes the human race so special, the ability to evaluate as a part of our awareness capabilities.

Most people waste their time by trying to find minor deals or how to cut corners when paying their taxes or bills. But what message are you sending to the Universe by doing that? You are saying that there is not enough. This doesn't mean you should avoid deals that are offered, valuable, or easy to get. But losing hours trying to save a few bucks is insane.

A long time ago, there was this guy I knew and he was buying a home sound system. He searched for hours where he could get the best deal for the set he liked. He ended up traveling to a neighboring city, spending hours in online search and travel. He also spent $20 on gas to save $40 altogether. In the meantime, he lost a client because he was late for his appointment.

Instead of searching for a better deal, I invest my time into ideas that will help me get more money. I am spending my energy regardless. So, instead of spending my time looking for small deals and saving, I am looking for another business opportunity, another business to start, another skill to attain, or how I can scale up my current businesses. Perhaps I can put up a new website, build a new app, upload some new tunes to iTunes, write a few more pages of my book. I get educated by taking new courses, classes, and tutorials so I can figure out how I can promote my business better. In general: I am investing my time in new skills, knowledge, and expansion of my existing businesses as well as building new ones. Not all deals are the same. Some are not worth your time.

Where is your focus ultimately? Are you trying to get a good deal buying a house, or are you wasting your time finding a cheaper pair of shoes online? You would be amazed how much time people spend to save a couple of bucks instead of refocusing their attention on how to acquire hundreds, thousands, even millions of dollars.

For some, paying bills isn't the most enjoyable activity, but I always put good energy into this responsibility because I am grateful to God that I have plenty, that I can pay, and I can give. What you put out, you create more of. If you put out joy that you are able to fulfill your duties, you will be blessed to do even more so.

Wouldn't it be wonderful if the Universe would just use you as a distributor, as a medium to get its money out, a bank let's say? A bank does not just save money. It provides jobs, loans, credits, and other services. But also remember, banks do not give out money for free. They might be donating to charities, but they do not give money to their friends just to make them look better.

So do not just show gratitude for what you get; show it for what you have to give.

By shifting your energy and changing focus, you get into the big game and vibrate on a higher energy. You orient your focus toward large deals rather than on pennies. Think big. Those who thrive financially don't waste an extra second fretting about how much their electrical or phone bill costs. But to get there, first you have to turn things around and live according to that mentality. You must tune in to the Universe's vibration of abundance. Be thankful that you can afford what you can—because by doing so, you are supporting one of the very best things for both your bank account and society at large: creating and supporting jobs.

Decide To Be Rich

Today, of course, money is indispensable. It's like a coat that keeps you warm in cold weather when you need that extra layer. If you have a very large coat, you can help cover others too. Without it, you will be freezing and can't focus on anything but the fact that you are cold, which distracts you from your true purpose—and it impedes achievement of your true potential. Once you are warm enough, you can start really living, developing ideas, and spreading your wings. When you get that struggle out of your way, you can go after your real potential.

Prolific inventor and entrepreneur Elon Musk who brought us: PayPal, a simple way to transfer money instantly over the Internet; Tesla cars, the first fully reliable and functional commercial cars that run entirely on electric power; and many other ventures. He is said to have decided to live on a mere dollar a day for some time back in his late teens. He did it so he would be able to develop—or at least to figure out—his business potential. This was Musk's way of determining how to get a warm enough coat so he could then concentrate on going after what he wanted.

Once you take care of what you need, you can focus on what you *want*. You should not pursue money; *it* should go after *you*. And this starts to happen only after you become independent of it.

Think of it like a circle spinning round. You're in that circle, chasing money around and around, but if you can somehow stop your motion and reverse course, money will be chasing *you*. And when you figure out how to reverse that loop, you begin to figure out much more important things.

You see, everything that you are looking for is around you all the time, but if you don't pay attention, you won't be able to see it.

Giovanni was invited one day to his boss's house with another three coworkers. As they all walked through the yard together, on their way, under their feet, was a water hose unrolled. Everybody, except Giovanni, just stepped over it. However, Giovanni rolled it back. That got his boss's attention and soon enough as his boss was giving him more responsibilities, Giovanni progressed rapidly through the company. The truth of the matter was that the boss had left that hose intentionally unwound to see who would pay attention to it. Giovanni was paying attention and therefore was rewarded.

Chapter Five:
Action

The Magician

Meet Eric. Eric worked as a security officer at an apartment complex, but his passion was magic. Every weekend, Eric would go to the city square to perform magic. His most famous act was being tied up with a rope by a few audience members. The only rule they had to follow was not to go under his belt or clothes with the rope. No matter how the audience members tied Eric up, he would manage to break loose in less time than it took to restrain him. After the act, he would hold his hat out for donations and reap the rewards from a delighted audience.

One day as Eric was guarding the housing complex, a young teen from one of the houses threw chairs into the pool. Eric caught the kid and took him to his mom, who wanted to punish him. However, Eric proposed taking the kid with him to the city square to help him perform the tricks instead. The mother agreed.

So Eric and the teen went to the city square that weekend. When it came time for Eric to perform the rope trick, the kid proposed to the audience to blindfold Eric during the trick. Eric was petrified and tried to object; but the audience gave their enthusiastic approval. The teen blindfolded Eric, and several members of the audience started to tie up Eric with the rope. Eric was scared to death, unsure if he would be able to pull off his trick this time.

As they finished tying him up, it was time for Eric to free himself. He noticed that despite his instructions, someone had also tied the rope to his belt. Eric was shaking, but he started anyway. The audience watched with rapt attention. Finally, he managed to break loose and free himself from the rope, as he was not really tied to his belt; the kid just tucked a piece of rope into his belt to make it appear so. By that time, the crowd had swelled to an impressive size. When Eric passed around his hat, he got more money than he ever had before.

Often, we get upset by apparent obstacles that the Universe puts in front of us, unaware that they are actually for our benefit. What appear to be setbacks or impediments are in fact opportunities. To do the trick with greater success—and therefore reap a greater monetary reward than he ever had before—Eric had to take advantage of an unexpected change and perform the trick in a new way. To get something you never had before, you have to be willing to do something you have never done before.

Only The Brave

Action requires courage. I wish I could tell you that you can just sit back, relax, imagine, and visualize and it will appear to you magically. But that's not the case. A little baby feels warm, cozy, and provided for in its mother's womb. It grows there for about nine months, but in order to grow more, it has to leave that place of safety. It has to be born. Birth is for sure a huge shock for a baby. But that's how growth happens, through breakthroughs that are the results of taking action despite fear.

Everyone can be brave in victory, but maintaining character and courage in defeat separates champions from everyone else.

Getting money requires that you have the courage to believe in yourself. It means that you need to go against the grain when everyone is saying your idea is crazy—to be your true self when everyone else simply follows the predictable path, and to exhibit unflappable integrity when cheating and cutting corners is so easy.

It means having the courage to be unapologetic when everyone is opposing you, and to deal with the challenges of the day when something unexpected messes up your plans.

Finally, instead of complaining and pointing fingers, it takes courage to stay strong, to persevere, and to stand up for yourself. For instance, a bank must be trustworthy, well secured, and managed honestly so we can gain trust in it and deposit our money. The same way the Universe has to have its trust in us, so we can serve as a mediator; therefore, store your money for the Universe. As individuals, we can't be discouraged, quit all the time, or cry about all our woes either. The Universe will not reward any bank, business, or person who can be broken so easily.

Fear of losing can ruin relationships with people and money. Having money requires a certain amount of courage. But with practice, you can overcome fear and gain more courage. The more courage you show, the more the Universe is willing to trust you with more money.

It's a similar situation to conquering a fear of heights. You just take as many steps as you feel comfortable with—and each time move to a higher floor of a building once you start to feel good about the previous height. In this way, you slowly get used to going incrementally higher—and having more and more money. You also must have the courage to give, to seed—not just to gain for yourself.

Chapter Six:
Associations

Board The Airplane

Everyone who has ever flown on a plane is likely familiar with the safety instructions presented before every flight: in the event the oxygen masks drop down, put yours on first, then help others. The same principle applies to wealth. You probably know someone who has seen a motivational video, read a book, or attended a self-development seminar—and then runs around purporting to be an expert on the subject of money.

Chances are that you know people like this—those who try to help others but can't even help themselves. They know what is best for the rest of the world, but cannot run their own lives. Successful people know how to listen while others just want to get their point across. Some people believe that for them to succeed, everyone else has to change; their boss, their spouse, their friends. But there is only one corner of the Universe you can change: yourself. And by changing yourself, you change your entire universe. If you want to make it easier for your children, you have to make it for yourself first. By trying to correct others, we avoid working on ourselves. Children especially, often don't do what we tell them; they learn from the example we present to them.

Trying to do it the other way around, helping others before you make it yourself, is like building a house and giving your bricks away. Will you ever be able to finish your house if you are giving your bricks away in the middle of the process?

If people want to overcome addiction, they have to look for help, and most importantly, when they do look for help, they need to release not just their old habits but their old friends, and find some new ones—friends who support and encourage your progress, not those who try to hold you back. Going to therapy and, after therapy, meeting friends who encourage your misbehavior is going to perpetuate your addiction. The same is true of getting money. If you want to get married, would you hang around a singles crowd? Listening to their advice about relationships that keeps them where they are—single? If you want to become wealthy, would you accept financial advice from broke people? Odds are, if you hang around five broke people, you're most likely going to be the sixth, and if you hang around five rich people, you're most likely going to be the sixth. Your income is the average of the five people you associate with most of the time, so be selective about the company you keep. Sometimes you have to release the excess weight. Even on an airplane, you are not allowed to take more than two carry-on bags.

Once you start to shift your status in life, a gap emerges between you and those who have not shifted. And that is all right; not everyone is on the same journey as you. Some people will stay where they are; some will support you; and the best ones will join you and contribute. The ones who refuse to move because they feel too comfortable with their status may even feel rejected. But that is none of your concern. They have all the freedom to do what they please with their lives. You can only assist those who want to be assisted—and of course, yourself.

Who Are Your Friends?

In the early 1990's, there was an enormously huge hip hop superstar who, at the top of his career, challenged Michael Jackson to a dance competition. I was a big fan of his; I'd been listening to his music even before he became "big." As he became more popular, he hired more staff for his shows—trying to help out his friends, family, and peers by giving them jobs. The problem was, they weren't real jobs. After he hired all the dancers he could find, he was paying people just to stand on the stage with him. And soon enough, he went bankrupt. I can only imagine, once the paychecks stopped coming in, how quickly those people probably abandoned him.

As the saying goes: you can give a man a fish and feed him for a day; but if you teach him how to fish, you feed him for life. The Universe looks more favorably upon people who show others how to fish rather than just handing them out fish. The Universe wants us to grow, but growth requires action—and investing energy!

However, not every person is willing to learn how to fish. When you just hand out money to people, you are taking away the potential blessing they'll earn if they were to excel on their own. Instead, they become dependent on handouts instead of fulfilling their purpose.

When Andrew Carnegie, often identified as one of the richest people and Americans ever, funded the construction of libraries around the world, he would always make people participate, either by paying for the land or for books for the library. He didn't just pay for all of it. He felt that for people truly to appreciate something, they needed to invest in it. That's how you get them involved and that's how they value a gift.

You enable people when you give them a little push; but don't take the entire ride away from them by diminishing their purpose and experience.

Who are you surrounding yourself with? Do you keep people around merely because they're on your payroll, or are they part of the team? Do they contribute? You want to hire individuals who can and will generate some value for the business. To get ahead, you might need to release the excess weight and bring along people and investments that can drive prosperity.

And who are your friends? Do they add blessings and value to your life? Do they inspire you or drain you? Where, and with whom, do you invest life's most precious resource—your time? The most successful people invest in friends who inspire them and who are going somewhere. The biggest luxury in this world is the ability to waste time. People who know this invest their time wisely; they even multiply it by getting others to work for them.

If you really want to help others, instead of giving handouts, look to inspire them. And you can only inspire others if you become a better version of yourself.

Take Responsibility: Don't Feed The Bears

Have you ever seen a sign in a park that says "Don't Feed the Bears"? If people feed a bear too often, it loses its capability to feed itself when people are not around. Bears also become violent if one refuses to share their food. This has always reminded me of people who believe they are entitled to others' constant help and support.

Is there someone in your life who is always short on rent, or always needs a few extra bucks to buy something? And does someone—probably you—always come through to assist them? And it goes on and on like this with no end in sight?

Sometimes helping other people is like feeding the bears in that you're doing them more harm than good, despite your best intentions. There are exceptions, of course. People need a well-deserved push sometimes. But if this becomes a behavioral pattern, it means that person's subconscious had become programmed with the notion that someone else will *always* pick up the slack or bail them out.

These types of people constantly look for the answers outside of themself. They're looking for others to hand them something. They think that the people who "have" should share more, because they don't have enough. These are the kind of people who refuse to grow up. A grown-up person is not looking for discounts or help, paltry savings and negligible bargains that waste more time than they're worth for the small amount of money at stake.

People who are the opposite of this take destiny into their own hands. They do not complain or point fingers. They dress and talk properly, give respect first, and act appropriately for their age.

We all begin our lives the same way: needing to rely on others—our parents, mainly—for help. But relying on them for too long just inhibits us from reaching our full potential.

It's comfortable for people when others take care of them, but if you want to be rich, if you want to be independent, you have to grow up and take responsibility for your life.

One Thing

One thing that people desire more than anything, and I mean more than *anything*, more than money, power, or sex, is validation. Validation comes in many forms, as acceptance, recognition, gratification, and acknowledgment, for instance. Most people seek that validation for who they are and what they do. If they can't put forward anything of greater value to get validated, such as education, title, or other accomplishments, people often brag about their nationality or what group they belong to. In any case, people strive to get validated.

This desire goes back to ancient history. In order to survive, you had to be a part of a tribe; and to be part of a tribe, you had to be accepted. If you were not accepted from the start, even as a baby, you couldn't survive if your parents rejected you. But here's the catch: if you demonstrated *too* much skill, you might have been selected as a village champion. This meant that if your village was attacked, they might send *you* to fight the attacker's champion or to lead a battle and risk life and limb putting yourself out there. So the goal was to be acceptable—but not extraordinary.

That mechanism keeps people average even to this day, keeping them mired in a loop of mediocrity. How many people do you know talk about how they are going to do this or that, yet do nothing to move forward—even for years? When they do try to break through, as soon as someone else notices their progress or even intention and recognizes them for it, they pull back. As soon as they convince others that they have a great plan or idea and receive praise for it, they stop. This process repeats ad infinitum.

One of the reasons why average people can't surpass "average" is because they have to be validated constantly. And they'll spend all their money and time just searching for that validation. Some people spend all their money on expensive designer clothes but don't even have a retirement plan in place. They flash their fancy cars but have no furniture at home.

Why do you think so many people want to be actors, models, or singers? Wherever you live, I bet you know at least a dozen people pursuing success in these competitive fields—because fame is a form of gratification. *Everybody* strives to be liked and accepted; we just have different ways to attract other people's attention. Some people are smarter about it, while others will do just about anything. And the same reason it is risky to become the tribe's champion is why it is risky to become a celebrity. Therefore, our subconscious does everything possible to protect us— even self-sabotage!

In the 2004 movie *Troy,* the character Achilles, played by Brad Pitt, provides a very good example of a champion. At the very beginning of the movie, Achilles is called in the name of King Agamemnon of Mycenae to fight Bogarius, the champion of King Triopas of Thessaly's troops. Achilles is pretty much a rock star of the ancient world; but there is a price to pay for that. A constant danger for his life. What looks dandy and glorious on the big screen is not so illustrious in real life. Would you jeopardize your life like that? Few people have that kind of courage. That's why only a few have what they have and do what they do.

You see, if Achilles had only a bit of doubt in himself, his subconscious would advise him to run for cover. *You* have to run *it*; don't let *it* run *you*.

What's Your Story

So, if fear of change is the only thing standing between you and your success, you must eliminate the story that's holding you back. Everyone has an "autobiography", a personal narrative they use to define who they are. No matter where you come from, your past likely has instances of hardship or even abuse. I certainly have my own. However, this is not what I allow to define me; I have left it in the past, where it belongs.

It's hard for many to leave their stories behind. Their story is bound up in their identity, their sense of self, who they are. And it's often what gets other people's attention. It's how they elicit sympathy. It's how they attract love. Take away their story, and they don't have anybody to blame for their shortcomings. They have to face themselves in the mirror.

Whatever you consciously choose will be what's real to you. Whatever your predominant daily thoughts are will be your reality. So why not choose to be happy and wealthy?

People tend to listen to what they already believe; they subconsciously seek out information that supports their views. This tendency is called "confirmation bias"—and it's a very limiting way of navigating the world. Some people, when they pick their political candidate, will look for any and every proof they can find that they are the right one and the opposition is wrong. Everything negative about that candidate would be discarded or justified immediately by those people. Usually, what you have in your life at any given point is in exact alignment with your beliefs. If you believe that everything is easy, that's how you see the world. And if you believe it's a struggle to achieve anything in this life, you will find all the proof to back up your beliefs. We see the world through our filters; and we have to filter everything to fit our preset beliefs. This keeps us from disrupting our subconscious.

People are creating all the time. We are delivering results all the time. Either we build or we tear down. The next step is to figure out how to be successful in what you would like to have, not what you would like *not* to have—to be successful in how to make money, instead of just how to get by.

Consider this story: A long time ago, Leon was with a group of Boy Scouts camping in the woods. They were carrying out an exercise where they had to maintain silence for 48 hours and write down their thoughts and goals in life. They had to set up their tents at least thirty feet apart so they wouldn't interact with each other. It was a rainy day and the spots some of the Scouts were assigned were on the side of the hill, so the ground was uneven.

Leon pitched his tent in the rain and settled in. But since the ground beneath him was sloping downward, he would roll down each time he tried to sleep, landing where rainwater was creating a small pond inside his tent. Frustrated, Leon decided to move the tent a few yards away to a flat surface while remaining respectful to obey the rules and to be far enough away from neighboring tents.

The rest of the time he spent there was very fruitful. He became inspired and wrote some great ideas in his book. It was a breeze for him, a really pleasant and enlightening experience.

Later on, it was time for everyone to gather round and share their experiences. Some of the Scouts shared stories about how they struggled and it was hard because the terrain was uneven for most of them and there was the rain and all sorts of other challenging things. Yet none of them moved from their locations because they wanted to tell stories of how it was hard yet they still managed to overcome it all by not giving up and trying to improve their position. That fueled their inspiration. They wanted to have stories that would give them validation of their hardships. Leon wanted a solution.

This story provides proof about how easy it is to change a small thing—like moving to another place, or spot on the hill—and how that can improve your life and clarify your perspective. Of course, some people need to have their struggle stories. They have to come up with attention-catching excuses as to why this endeavor did not work for them. But not Leon; he was a happy camper!

So what do you prefer? To share your story of struggle as an excuse—or to enjoy instant success with very little effort? People frequently overlook how critical it is to have a good starting position in order to speed up their success. It can be as simple as moving from one neighborhood to another—or even one room to another. We can move past our struggles by making a simple move; yet some people tend to stay put simply to support the story they've created for themselves, a story that serves only to get others' attention and validation. Either you have your own negative stories or positive results. When you have good results, others do the talking for you and about you.

I used to own a *Windows*-based PC, and I was so proud to be able to install my own drivers for each component of the machine. I would go to the graphic card manufacturer's website and download the newest drivers. Then, I would do the same thing for the CD drive and other components like antivirus software, ways to tweak up a machine for better performance, and all sorts of other time consuming things. Now, I look back and think of what a waste of time that was! I could have done so much more instead of being proud for that completely useless skill that would just mercilessly consume my time and keep me from my work.

I would rather have a car that never breaks than be a skillful mechanic with a car that breaks all the time, unless being a mechanic is my calling. Why not stretch a few dollars more and buy a more reliable computer or car, something that has a great track record of being self-sufficient and reliable? Do you ever think back to the things you had to master in the past that are totally useless today? Sometimes we create our own completely unnecessary challenges.

People often think that their struggle is evidence that they can present to the Universe to ask for compassion and help. Even if they don't ask God directly for compassion, they think God sees everything sooner or later and is going to come to their rescue. The truth is—the Universe communicates with us all the time, if we would just put our struggles aside for a moment and listen. By placing his tent in a better, more comfortable position, Leon had time to relax and to listen to the Universe and to God's word. A struggle is not necessarily part of your success. It's not about life happening to you; it's about life happening *from and for* you.

Chapter Seven:
Habits

The Protection Mechanism

Our Subconscious Mind's main task is to keep us safe, even if it means keeping us away from our greatness. This can make the subconscious one of the biggest obstacles to our success. Novelty scares the Subliminal Mind, causing us to resist the unknown even if the path to success runs *through* the unknown. Our Subconscious Mind discourages us from taking risks. And even when we take a risk and gain something, it will try to talk us out of it because it wants to keep us safe. Often, people remain stuck in dead-end jobs or unhealthy relationships merely because they feel "safe". The familiar is often less scary than the unknown, even if what is familiar is bad for us.

Imagine that the Subconscious Mind is your parent, and you are a kid asking to ride a bike. You've never ridden a bike before and your parents want to keep you safe from falling and hurting yourself. How do you convince your parents to let you ride that bike? If you're like most kids, by *constantly asking*. Then you make progress by starting small—maybe riding it just in your driveway—until your parents begin to feel comfortable with the idea.

Now, imagine that you took a bike and just went riding it down the street without permission. You took a risk. When you came back home, your parents were upset. They would not let you ride that bike again, at least for some time.

That's why there are so many short-term successes, like one-hit wonders, that fizzle before panning out into anything of substance.

Break out of that comfort zone and take a risk. Ride that bike. Consider the three possible outcomes:

1) Never try it and keep your parents (subconscious) at peace;

2) Try it and then quit (quick, fleeting success that does not last);

3) Convince your parents over a period of time until they begin to feel comfortable with the idea (vision boards, affirmations).

Or *just do it*, and don't give up until you succeed and show your parents that you are just fine and that they can rest assured knowing you can ride that bicycle on the street. This is a quantum leap, but you have to be willing to feel uncomfortable for a longer period of time before your subconscious becomes accustomed to the change.

That self-talk that you hear all the time is your inner parent trying to talk you out of doing whatever new and scary thing you're trying to do. Remember, its primary function is to keep you safe—whether you're happy or not. That's why you need to take time to talk to your parents while also taking action.

That's the same reason why saving work for other people is a means of acquiring wealth. By saving little by little, your subconscious is getting used to the idea of having more.

Now imagine a long ago time, when the world was a much less safe place. You just got yourself a pile of money, gold if you wish. You carry that gold with you as you travel, even though you know that there is a chance of being robbed and even losing your life for the gold that you carry while you're en route. You have two options: release the gold to save your life, or arm yourself and muster the courage to confront villains.

The real question is: can you persevere through the pressure? Can you take responsibility? We don't win because we back away, or if are saying to ourselves "what was I thinking? I don't have skills/vitality/brains. I am not smart enough/educated enough/lucky enough/young enough/old enough" (or whatever you might think is your disadvantage).

You shouldn't go cruising down the hill without brakes on your bike, but challenging yourself and stretching your beliefs can take you a long way.

Some people have never dealt with millions of dollars, so imagine if they got their hands on that amount of cash. Their subconscious likely would find a way to take it from them to keep them safe, just like taking a pack of matches from a child who wants to play with fire. Just read what happens to most lottery winners. However, this also works the other way around. If you are used to having millions, that is your safe haven—so if you lose those millions, they *have* to come back. That's the reason why people raised in wealth have a wealthy mindset, and why children of wealthy parents are more likely to stay that way. That's why if you hang around rich people, some of that "magic" might brush off on you.

Your Innate Reflex

In order for humans to survive, our subconscious has to develop certain mechanisms that trigger our reflexes. So when our prehistoric ancestors were facing danger, and a split second meant the difference between life and death, their reflexes made sure that they would react promptly to survive.

We possess an unimaginable number of those preset subconscious loops that basically run our lives. Those programs begin to operate as soon as we come into this world and are shaped by our environment, in concert with genetics. We are influenced by everything around us, starting with our parents, then siblings, extended family, friends at school, and so forth. Those "inner programs" are created basically in two ways: either through repetition; or as the result of an intense emotional event that became stuck in our subconscious. The saying goes that a person who gets burned by a bowl of steaming hot soup then will blow even on cold a glass of water, expecting it to be hot. I once put a cup of milk in a microwave oven to warm it up. Little did I know that some dishes are not microwavable so as I grabbed it to take it out, I burned my fingers. Since then, every time I take something out of a microwave, I touch it carefully to test first. I got programmed to that habit by that first painful experience.

Those programs dictate our behavior. But with sustained, concentrated effort, we can mold our subconscious programming into something else. When I was in elementary school, I had a very good friend named John who was pretty much like every other kid. But when we started fourth grade, he suddenly started to act goofier. He wanted to be a funny type of guy. I vividly remember how at first it looked just like an act to me—and I could not stand it! He was my good friend, and I knew his real nature, and this was *not* it. But miraculously, after six months or a year later, that goofy persona became his actual character, and I accepted it. I started to believe it and to see him as such: the funny, entertaining, class clown. John is still that guy today. Very early in life, I discovered that if someone adapts to a role long enough, the "role" can solidify into one's actual personality. It's an example of changing one's programming by repetition.

If someone is raised in an environment where money is scarce—and perhaps even a constant cause of tension between their parents or other family members—that person will develop certain attitudes about money, perhaps that money is something that shouldn't be discussed, or that leads to unpleasant conversations. These attitudes will "program" subconsciously how this person acts towards money.

Your conscience is a gatherer of information, feelings, and tools that are stored into your subconscious, which then execute on autopilot. These preset reflexes run your life without you even actively thinking about it.

The good news is that we can reset this "autopilot" mode and change our settings. Think of your mind like a Smartphone, and watch closely what type of apps you are installing on it!

Remember, our subconscious is here to protect us by any means necessary. So until we change, we can never hide who we really are, since our autopilot takes over and reveals our true self every time.

Interrupt The Pattern

The self-preserving nature of the subconscious is strong. By the time you read this, your subconscious programs have been reinforced by a lifetime of repeated behavior. Changing this behavior—disrupting or perhaps "uninstalling" those programs—necessitates *re*programming. This is made difficult in part by the discomfort that comes with change. But in order to grow, we must keep challenging ourselves, we must keep refining our abilities.

One way to break the pattern could be to begin doing everything you think about in a different way when possible. It may be as simple as using a different hand for certain tasks, leaving your office through a different exit, parking your car at a different parking spot, or engaging people in conversations you normally wouldn't approach. For example, people ask, "Hi, how are you today?" The uninspired response is usually, "Good, thanks, how about yourself?" Why not use your imagination and come up with something different? For example: "My day was amazing so far; I hope yours was too, sir/madam." Try to come up with something original (but of course, appropriate, respectful, light, and harmless.)

If you are the one who usually pays when you go out with your friends, don't do it next time. Conversely, if you always share the bill, try to treat your friends for a change. Take your usual behavior and start doing it the other way around. Challenge yourself. *Learn to feel comfortable being uncomfortable.* What is the biggest tip you've given to a service person? What was the biggest amount you've donated to a charity? Try something out of your comfort zone. And when you do it, *own* it. Do not brag about it, and do not get all shook about it. You need to own it.

By trying something new on a regular basis, your life can shift tremendously. You'll gain new perspectives and new perspectives attract new opportunities.

The significance doesn't lie merely in *what* you do, but in how you *feel* about doing it. Nothing actually has meaning until you give it meaning. And that meaning creates your own reality—what it represents to you. One person can have what they believe is a convincing argument for their particular point of view, while another person might use all those same arguments to claim a completely opposite reality. If I have a thousand dollars in my pocket, you might say I have the freedom to buy what I want and be grateful for it. Or you might claim that a thousand dollars is not nearly enough for what I would like to get. One might say that our country is free because we have a government, military, and police to protect us—while another person might claim that these forces exist to ensure the opposite of freedom, to control or to oppress us. It's all a matter of perspective. If two people are standing across from each other at a number six displayed on the ground, one person will claim it's a six—and the guy across from him will claim it's a nine!

The good news is, if you can reshape your own reality, you can change your results. It's not an instantaneous process, of course; but if you are persistent, your reality eventually can become whatever you make of it.

Chapter Eight:
Thoughts

The Mind

If you don't take control of your mind, others will. Are you truly aware of what is going through your mind every day? What do you read, watch, and listen to on a daily basis?

Remember: our brains are made up of a conscious, subconscious, and Universal Mind. The Universal Mind is kind of like the collective consciousness, the totality of everyone's minds combined.

We already know that our subconscious' task is our preservation; it keeps us safe, as often we wish for things that we don't really want or that are contrary to our interests. Every thought that we have is like a small wish. It's estimated that we have some 50,000 to 70,000 thoughts per a day. Now, imagine if every one of those thoughts would go directly to the Universal Intelligence. It would be chaos. Fortunately, our guardian angel, in the form of our Subconscious Mind, asks every time, "Are you sure about that?"

Every time we have a thought, it's "stamping" the subconscious. And the more we stamp it with the same thing, the more the message gets out to the Universal Mind, which eventually delivers what we ask for. That's how and why affirmations, vision boards, goal cards, and prayers can be effective—just by repeating the same thing over and over again and/or holding an image in your head for a long period of time. It has no choice but to be delivered, whether beneficial or detrimental to us.

If we repeatedly impress upon our subconscious some thought or desire, it eventually will connect with the Universal Mind. This repetition of the same thing upon our subconscious can be active or passive, intentional or unintentional. Affirmations, visualizing, prayers, or any active repetition that we consciously engage in is intentional. Being surrounded by the same things on a daily basis is unintentional conditioning. That's why people tend to remain in their current situation. Whatever you surround yourself with is going to rub off on you eventually.

So why not attract what you really want? Why not decide consciously to repeat to yourself what you would really like to achieve? Why not find encouraging friends, or move to a better neighborhood? Why not hang out at better places, restaurants, plays, and theaters? Why get entertained by dramas and crime movies instead of funny comedies and enlightening shows? Why eat junk food instead of delicious healthy meals?

We can bridge the gap between our minds and the Universal Mind through *concentration and repetition*. Most people are prone to distraction; their thoughts are all over the place, and at the same time nowhere at all. They are looking to be entertained. They let life passively unfold on them, and they cannot stand a minute with themselves. They have to check their Smartphones instantly. They are disconnected.

In contrast, successful people concentrate their thoughts; they learn, listen, and have a definite goal backed up by a plan of action.

Get connected with your inner self. Seek guidance within yourself through to the Universe. Listen to your inner voice. The more you cancel the noise of the everyday world, the more clearly you'll be able to hear the voice inside you.

HOW TO GET MONEY

Illustration of The Mind

Illustration of The Mind Explanation

The first picture shows three minds.

C = Conscious Mind

S = Sub-Conscious Mind

U = Universal Mind

The picture shows how our surroundings influence our Conscious Mind. The arrows symbolize external influences, like education, environment, news, media, other people, and so on. Through the filters of our mind, our Conscious Mind then impacts our Sub-Conscious Mind; and our Sub-Conscious Mind transmits to the Universal Mind. In this way, your predominant thoughts are stamping continuously on your Sub-Consciousness Mind. Then, your Sub-Consciousness Mind orders delivery through the Universal Mind and creates your reality.

Manifestation

So—how *could* one manifest $1,000,000? To manifest, by the way, means "to bring about" or "to make real". The word is often used in the context of *attracting* some object of desire. Some people say it works, some say—not so much.

Say you would like to manifest a million dollars by repeating an affirmation. How long might it take to manifest it? Let's compare it to building a house, if it takes on average 10,000 bricks to build a nice house.

Let's say if every time you repeat the affirmation, you get a dollar for it. Wouldn't that be cool? You just say a sentence and one dollar appears. You say another one and another dollar comes into your hands. So you are about to manifest a million dollars in five years. Therefore, your affirmation sounds like this: "By (here insert the exact date five years from today), I am so happy and grateful now that I am a millionaire."

In order to repeat that a million times over the course of five years, you need to repeat the same sentence about 548 times each day for five years straight, without taking a day off. Writing that manifestation down 548 times a day would hold even greater weight. If that is what it takes to become a millionaire, would you do it?

I am convinced that if you did that, you would for sure manifest it. It would be imprinted into your subconscious like an engraving in stone. Not that merely repeating the words would magically make it happen; you'd be integrating it into your subconscious, you would force yourself to *find ways* to make it happen.

After you repeated it so many times, after it's stuck in your mind, you kind of get used to it. All of a sudden, it's not something distant to you; but rather something you have in your hand. Most of the successes that I have achieved in my lifetime snuck up on me. I was not even aware that I did it. Often I'd look back and be amazed by it. What seemed like a dream a year before was completely normal when I had it. To me, living in America was once just a dream. Walking by my favorite neighborhood picturing having a house there, used to be just a dream. Writing a book and buying a brand new car used to be just dreams for me. Having a computer used to be a big goal for me, later getting a laptop. Now I own half a dozen of those devices. And I am so grateful for all of it and much more as all this looks just normal to me today. What are some of the things in your life that you hardly could believe you could get or achieve in the past and today you are so grateful for them because they are just a part of your life today? Is it that dream job, dream house, dream car, dream relationship, or dream partner?

Dreams tend to manifest when your fear of failure becomes bigger than your fear of success. Remember: you are repeating this mantra to your subconscious—and its job is to keep you safe by any means necessary. By repetition through time, you are convincing it that you will become safer with your goal than without it. I see repetition of manifestations like scratching your fingernail on a wooden board. The more you scratch it at the same spot, the closer you are to breaking through eventually. It just takes commitment.

Synchronization

People who are what I call "in sync" get better results. When a person is stressed, angry, or resentful, they are out of sync. The Conscious and Subconscious Mind—and perhaps also the mind and body—are not communicating as they should. That causes various unwanted results, including physical illness. It's as if three people are trying to build a house and each one is doing something that actually interferes with the task of the other two. One is laying bricks while another one is yelling, "Hey, the foundation is not laid right! We have to take down this wall!" Meanwhile, the third guy is digging up the ground.

Spending time with yourself is helpful because it is like giving instructions to those three workers so they are clear about the process and goals and can be in sync with each other. This is also why vision boards and affirmations are necessary: for mapping, for laying out your plan for your builders.

Do you have a plan of your goal written down?

Your Inner Treasure Chest

We all have something I call our inner "treasure chest"—that is, the average amount of money we have at any given time. Have you ever noticed that no matter how much you earn, you tend to end up with about the same amount in the end? You may see a change—either upwards or downwards—over a longer timeline; but how often do you come into some money, only to run into some unforeseen problem or opportunity that forces you to spend what you just gained? In the end, the net gain/loss is zero. The phenomenon can work the other way around, too: some emergency comes your way and you have no clue where the money is going to come from, but somehow it is manifested.

How many times have you heard about a rich man who goes broke and then becomes rich again? Or famous athletes who end up bankrupt only a few years after their athletic career ends? Or lottery winners who eventually lose everything they won—or even end up in debt? That's their inner "treasure chest," their default status, their "homeostasis," to borrow a term from biology. Some feel comfortable having it all; others feel uncomfortable with that idea. Some are used to plenty; others are not. That's your internal auto-preserving mechanism, taking you back to "baseline"—to your safe place with just enough money to get by. That's how most people live.

So you don't get more money merely by making more money; you do so by *expanding your treasure chest, your earning capabilities.* If the size of your treasure chest is $10,000 a month, then everything that exceeds that amount will stay outside of the chest—and odds are, the wind will blow it away. Conversely, if you feel a deficit in your "treasure chest," you will feel uncomfortable with the situation and your inner self will start to figure it out to make up for it. That's exactly why if someone who is accustomed to a certain level of wealth is suddenly bankrupt, they cannot feel comfortable or content with their new situation; every molecule in their body will yearn to fill up that "treasure chest" once again. Remember, growth starts from discomfort—from a restless sense that something is out of order and needs correction.

But let's imagine someone who is *not* used to a lot of money somehow coming into sudden wealth. If our subconscious works to maintain a feeling of stability or security, then squandering all that excess money is that person's way of "keeping safe".

That chest wind will blow away anything extra. So why not turn it around and start to *feel good* about getting more? *It's all how you feel about it.* Not what you or someone else thinks it is, but the meaning *you* assign to it. Our emotions dictate our results, and we are shaped by our predominant thoughts.

The size of your inner treasure chest usually correlates with the level of your stress threshold. In other words—what amount of money does it take to get your emotions going? Is it $1,000 or $10,000,000? If you had a chance to win $100,000,000, how would you react? Would you keep your cool—or would your brain be overloaded with adrenaline? Would it break you?

You get what you feel comfortable with and worthy of having. But comfort can be dangerous and deceiving when it leads us to be content with living beneath our potential, just because it's safe and familiar. To climb out of that loop, you must challenge yourself. You must expand your treasure chest to allow that auto-preserving system to grow and to expand. Otherwise, you get stuck with what you've always had.

So—how do you do that? By stepping out of the box you've put yourself in; by changing perspective; by challenging yourself and feeling comfortable about making changes.

If you are like me, you like getting great results while only spending a minimum of time and effort. You'd prefer good things to come to you instead of having to chase them.

Whatever keeps attracting your attention is your baseline level. The Universe has been rewarding you consistently up to a level that you're impressed by—and nothing higher. Do not try to impress others actively; just let your personality and achievements unfold by themselves. Don't *tell* people your goals, *show* them your goals. If you find that you are *too* impressed by anything out there, you are sending a subconscious message to the Universe that you are not worthy of having that thing.

The Trap

The Public Relations and media are giving enough material to people to keep their mind idle and totally preoccupied with useless information. The news does not serve only to inform you. It's primary purpose is ratings. And by serving what gets your attention, they earn ratings and an equivalent monetary reward.

No one is above you and no one is below you. We might be on different paths, but we are all equal. The moment you start to put some people on a pedestal, you essentially are saying that they're better than you. And then to maintain some kind of balance, you declare that other people must be *beneath* you. We know that you cannot help others before first improving yourself. The standard of living humanity enjoys today is better than at any time in history, and presumably it will only get better. You have to play your part. It isn't your job to save everyone; rather, it is to start with you and then continue with those closest to you. When we put ourselves together, everything else falls into place.

To get rich, you have get to a place where you feel like you do not owe anything to anyone and no one owes you anything. Guilt and resentment are invisible forces, but their effect is to keep people under control. Beware of people who try to convince you that the world needs saving. There are doubtlessly things we could work on; but overall, the world is grand and humans are a blessing to Mother Earth.

As of 2016, the worldwide average life expectancy was around 80 years. That means many people will live to be 90 years old and above. Life expectancy has *nearly doubled* over the past one hundred years. In 1986, half of the population's life expectancy was about 50 years of age. For the first time, less than 10% of the population today lives under the absolute level of poverty. And more people live under democracy than dictatorship. It's far from perfect and it probably never will be; but humanity is advancing by leaps and bounds.

They say that we do not inherit the Earth from our parents; we borrow it from our children. But our forefathers came up with vaccines, cures, medications, and all sorts of improvements. We would not be where we are now if they had not had the ingenuity and tenacity to invent trains, cars, machines, tools, and instruments, and to build roads, highways, bridges, and dams. We must thank them for that by doing our part by developing the things that we will leave to our sons and daughters when they take the reins from us.

HOW TO GET MONEY

Chapter Nine:
Discipline

It's A Marathon, Not A Sprint

People tend to perform contrary to the notion of commitment—which requires patience and dedication over the long term—and instead, act impulsively. Often, when someone wants to improve something in their life, they give everything they have to it for a week. Then they get exhausted and frustration sets in, at which time they give up because "it's not working". Well, it takes thousands of bricks to build a house. Just because you laid a few hundred in only a week's time doesn't mean that the rest of the house will build itself.

I used to be an avid runner. When you run a marathon, you don't sprint right at the beginning. You save your energy for the last stretch. Most people start marathons by sprinting and then give up when they soon get winded. It makes them look great for a minute, when they're out ahead of the crowd and get all the attention, but they almost never finish the race. Those people go from marathon to marathon, doing the same thing—just like some people go from project to project, from goal to goal, without pacing themselves and making it to the end.

There are three basic ways to run a marathon. One is the aforementioned "starting with a sprint". The second way is to sprint, then stop to catch your breath, then sprint again and catch your breath again. This approach is akin to those people who are frustrated with whatever they do, but they believe that raw persistence only will produce results. Persistence *is* good; but it takes us much farther if we also can adjust our plan and learn how to grow in the process. People often find themselves stuck in the same position, looking for a miracle to save them. But they tend not to realize that this "miracle" comes to the third type of runners.

The third type of runners start at a steady pace. They're aware of their advantages, but also of their limitations. They don't care about instant praise. They don't drain all their energy in a quick and flashy burst of speed just to gain attention from spectators. They aren't distracted by surroundings and circumstances. They create their own circumstances. They can't change the track itself, of course; but they know how to adjust. And when this type of runner approaches the end of the race, they have enough energy left to sprint to the finish line for the medal.

Most of life's bystanders only see the last few yards of that race—where a runner engages their sprint mode, eliciting comments from the crowd about how lucky that person must be. That's how it appears to people who have never even tried. They cannot see that it took this third runner twenty years of commitment to become what seems to be an "overnight success".

Ninety-two percent of people are bystanders; six percent are number one type runners; three percent are number two type runners; and *only one percent* are number three type runners. The sooner you learn how to run like the third runner, the sooner you can become a champion of marathons. A champion of getting money.

How Do You Attract Love

We all need love and attention. But it's important not to confuse real love (i.e., meaningful relationships cultivated over a long period of time) for shallow approbation (i.e. getting "likes" on a Facebook post). We're conditioned to seek attention from birth, because we have needs to be fulfilled. We need to be kept safe, fed, cleaned, protected—and when we're brought into this world, we don't know better than to cry. As a newborn baby, quickly we realize if we cry, our parents pay attention and then they come to check which one of ours needs has to be fulfilled. As we grow, we learn more sophisticated methods of getting attention. Additionally, being a part of the tribe requires that we establish our value and get a certain amount of attention so that we know our fellow tribesmen will come to the rescue in the face of danger. As we grow up, we tend to become more independent.

Unfortunately, not all people grow up. Some are in a constant search for attention, for instant gratification—and for some people, it becomes an addiction! If they get likes or comments on their social media posts and photos, they feel fulfilled. If they just get a great idea and talk to a few people about it and get their attention, their job is done.

But there is no substitute for actual work. It doesn't necessarily have to be *hard* work, but it has to be *targeted*, focused, and meaningful work. Even a thousand likes or comments are only play if they don't bring any material compensation. Only children do things for the sake of fun. Grown people need to have tangible results.

Now, imagine if you could find something that's fun for you, but also provides a lot of value for others and you get compensated for it.

No matter who you are, where you are, or what you do, we all have methods of attracting love, attention, and gratification. But in order really to excel in life, one must not get caught up in the game of instant gratification, but be ready to commit to bring something really great to this planet.

There are two basic ways to fulfill our need for love. The first one is by taking, asking, even blackmailing. That's the first one we learn as we are brought into this world. We cry, we wail, we irritate our parents or other caretakers until they fulfill our needs.

After some time, we learn how to find gratification by giving. Maybe we've just learned to walk. We give to our mother a flower that we picked out in the yard, and we get rewarded by a smile and a hug. Some people, however, will do anything to get that attention—even to the point of hurting themselves or others. They reason that this behavior will force someone else to take care of them thereby allowing them to shift their responsibilities to another person. After all, it gives them entitlement to their excuse. Successful people don't waste too much time in a pity party, they take responsibility and own their lives.

Postponing Gratification

Would you rather receive a million dollars today, or a million point five in six months? If I give you a million dollars in your hands right now and tell you if you come back in six months with the entire million—to the cent—I will give you one point five million, would you make it?

There have been many tests that look at the practice of postponing gratification conducted in the last and this century. In the Stanford Marshmallow Experiment conducted in the late 1960's, a child receives a marshmallow along with the promise that if they wait and don't eat it for fifteen minutes, they will get another one. Some children resisted the temptation; some took small bites and/or licks of the first marshmallow; and some simply could not wait and ate it. When follow-up studies were conducted in the early 1990's, the researchers discovered that the ability to delay gratification correlated with higher SAT scores.

The same theory applies when you can exhibit a little bit of discipline and commitment. Turn off that TV, put away that Smartphone, skip a few gossip parties, and put some work into your future. Your future-self will be very grateful to you. You reap today what you sowed five and ten years ago. It *sounds* a lot like a sacrifice. But whatever you sow today, you will reap the benefits five and ten years down the road. If you forego just a little bit more today, the *you* in five years will be grateful to the present *you*. You can live in the moment, but still work for the future.

Mental Exercises

People usually expect one big thing to change their life. But according to my experience and observation, all real changes come gradually, by implementing one change at a time, or should I say upgrading one thing at a time. Render slightly more services to your customers than you used to, buy just a little bit higher quality of shoes than previously, eat a better quality of food, or read one more book than you usually do, and so on. It's not about one big thing but rather hundreds—even thousands—of small tweaks. What you do is not nearly as important as what you become in the process of doing it. You see, what you do on a daily basis is shaping you. Now the question is, are you going in the direction of increase or decrease. One small change at a time rolls into a big snowball over time and causes avalanches. Now, which side of the hill are you rolling your snowball down, the wealth side or the other side of the hill?

One important thing that a person should eliminate is the 90% mentality. The latest statistics show that about 10% of the population holds almost 76% of the World's wealth? Abandon their 90% vocabulary and their 90% reasoning and excuses. Don't hang out with people who are talking about nothing. Instead, find some new friends with a different vocabulary—ones who exude and signify success. Spend time with people who refrain from trash talking and instead encourage others. Get involved in activities and clubs wherever you can find successful people. Study them.

Change your language, and your world will transform. If you are dedicated to be wealthy, you have to start to speak wealth. Your vibe attracts your tribe. So what kind of tribe would you like to attract?

Your beliefs, not the economy, dictate your success. Your mindset dictates your circumstances, not the other way around.

Your life is like an echo. Whatever you shout or even whisper out there, comes right back at you. If you are empowering and uplifting others, that's what comes right back at you. If you speak defeat, that's what's coming back to you and if you speak victory, that's what is coming back to you.

Imagine that whatever you do for yourself, the Universe will match and overflow. For every improvement in the quality of your life you achieve, the Universe doubles it.

Discipline Is The Money Magnet

In scientific terms, an object becomes "attractive" as it concentrates and lines up positive or negative electrons on one side. If an object has all its protons and electrons all over the place, it does not attract anything in particular. It takes order to supercharge efficiency.

In a similar way, when a person concentrates all their focus and intention on a definitive goal, there is no other outcome but for that person to start attracting the object of their thoughts, attention, and vision. If their focus is negative, they will attract negative things. If it's positive, good things will come. So, when someone is looking for excuses and says how something is impossible because such and such, that's *exactly* what that person will attract. If a person's focus is all over the place, actions will be all over the place and never be accomplished. If you start a job and let yourself be distracted by TV or social media or whatever, then the job is delayed not just for the time while your mind wandered away, but you'll have to add the time that it will take for you to regain your focus once more.

A person can think all day about money, but if that person thinks negatively about it, they will attract unfavorable results. If a person thinks all day about how they can't afford this or that or how they're not going to have enough, that person becomes a magnet for such outcomes.

Ask yourself: what type of electrons are you lining up? Positive or negative? Limiting or liberating? What are you disciplined about? Do you focus on complaints or solutions? Which side of yours is in order—the positive one or the negative one?

So, how much money would you like to make this year? Can you write down the exact amount? You need to have a clear vision and execution plan that you follow and act upon—and you must be disciplined about it.

If you can master yourself, you can master almost anything.

The Power of Compound Interest

Compound Interest is the motor of this world.

In this world, compound interest goes both ways. Whatever you invest in steadily through time will grow, at a slower pace initially, but if you keep watering it and nourishing it, eventually it will flourish. And when it does, it is usually out of proportion.

Unfortunately, it also goes the other way around. Whatever you neglect and don't give enough care to, through time it will consume you.

Everybody should know that you should go to the dentist at least every three to six months to clean your teeth and gums. There was this guy who had a toothache some time ago. He really did not trust dentists. I took him to a dentist and since he was neglecting his teeth and had poor hygiene, the dentist estimated $20,000 to fix everything. So, the guy did not trust the dentist and did not want to spend that kind of money and thought that he would be just fine. Just over a year later, two teeth fell out of his mouth. He panicked and returned to the dentist again. This time, the entire work was estimated to cost $50,000! The guy was very upset and went for a second opinion to another dentist. The second dentist gave him an estimate of $55,000!

There are people who are neglecting their houses, cars, and a lot of other things. A fix that could cost a few dollars today could turn easily to a penalty of thousands of dollars tomorrow.

All things are building up all the time. Some slower, some faster. But once when it catches you, it's much more work to fix.

As investing in yourself is the best thing you can do, you also have to be careful not to squander the little money that you have. Money loves money. The more you have, the more you get. But before you get to the "more" stage, you have to balance it out. You have to leave yourself a cushion, not just make emotional decisions foolishly.

HOW TO GET MONEY

Chapter Ten:
Faith

The Trapeze Theory

Once upon a time, Martin complained to a wise man that his business was struggling because he had poor-minded clients. Martin understood the difference between broke and poor-minded. His clients just had a poor mindset. At least, that's what Martin thought.

The wise man then asked Martin how long he could stay afloat if he lost all his clients. Martin responded that he had some savings and a small stream of income on the side so he could manage for a while without them. "Well, dear Martin," said the wise man, "then you need to jump. You have your safety net underneath, and you can't hold on any longer. As long as you keep those clients, there is no room for the clients you want to attract, because your current clients drain all your time and energy at the expense of possible higher quality clients. You need to create a need—a *vacuum*—that, by the Universe's law, demands to be filled in order to restore balance. So, you must take that chance and fill that vacuum with better customers."

To catch another trapeze, you have to let go of the previous one. But you also have to be sure that there's a safety net underneath you—and that the next trapeze is within your reach.

Whenever you let go of something, it leaves an emptiness that must be filled to retain the balance.

In order to get something you haven't had, you must give something you've never given. Yet that's what people resist the most. They'll give something up that they feel comfortable letting go of—but is that the right price? Remember the chapter "What is Currency" that talks about setting the price: if you keep getting the same results, then you're probably exchanging the same things in order to achieve them over and over again. And, as they say, "nothing ventured, nothing gained". Sometimes, you must take a real risk—and sacrifice something of real value—in order to reap a reward, scary as it may be.

Some people have precious silverware and dishes that they save for special occasions, or special clothing reserved only for major events. And yet those occasions rarely come, if ever. If not now, when will you live your life? What are you saving these things for? The only thing we have is now. The Universe gave us the present to use—not to collect dust. And why would the Universe give you more when you are not using your already attained gifts? To let them sit there in another drawer in your house?

Sometimes you need to release the excess weight in your life. Start with your own bedroom. Are you willing to go to your closet and get rid of your old clothes? Take out everything that you have not worn for over a year and give it away. Don't exchange it, don't sell it; just give it away. You will be surprised how quickly you will recoup your losses and your closet will be full again. When I wanted a new car, I got rid of the old one, just to create a vacuum that needed to be filled. I showed to the Universe that I was ready to receive the new car. I did everything in my power—and let the Universe take care of the rest. I got it much sooner than I had anticipated.

When you want new things, it is always a good idea to clear out the old stuff to create space for whatever is to come.

You have to let go in order to get something new. You have to give before you receive. Are you ready to release limiting beliefs, grudges, and habits that are not serving you? You need to get rid of all reminders of your previous relationships, people who let you down, to attract new ones. You need to clear up that energy so you can receive the new gifts that the Universe has in store for you. Physically and emotionally!

Ask, Act And It Shall Be Given To You

Ask the Universe for what you want like a child would ask a parent—boldly, but respectfully. Be repetitive. Show to the Universe with examples: go test-drive that car, call a realtor and go see that dream house, respectfully demand superb service at stores and exclusive shops—and keep being grateful at the same time. Feel what it would be like to own it, to be it, to have it.

There are two basic ways of communicating, the male and female version. The male version of communication is to say the point and expect that everything around that point to be self-explanatory. Men state the point and expect others to figure out the context or implication. The female version is to say everything around the point and expect the point to be self-evident.

When you talk to the Universe, your chances of being heard and granted the wish are better if you state clearly what you want and by *demonstrating* that you want it. In other words by using both methods of communication: the male and female. After all, how can one expect the Universe to bless them if the communication is unclear? Be to the point. How can one expect the Universe to provide that blessed and glorious life when one does not demonstrate a desire for it? Describe and explain, by getting emotionally involved about it. However, when you take care of yourself by example, the Universe *must* comply. When you drink water from a nice cup instead of a plastic bottle. When you have nice dishes and silverware instead of paper plates, pizza boxes, and plastic silverware. When you take care of your body and eat healthy, high quality foods. When you have your house in order and your car cleaned. When you buy yourself nice clothes. These are all forms of communicating to the Universe by example what you would like for yourself.

In order to become wealthy, you have to *feel* wealthy. You have to convince yourself that you've already "made it". And keep in mind all the while: the one you have to convince is yourself, not others!

Now meet Jack. Jack was always an above average person. He noticed how most of the things that he desired in his past somehow would manifest down the road. He adored a certain model of car and after some years, he acquired the exact one. But the thing was that he got the 1999 model of the car in 2005. He also noticed the same pattern with many other things. For example, he moved to a new neighborhood, an average, middle class American one. Jack would often walk to the grocery store and pass this beautiful, chic-looking housing complex. He was thinking to himself how awesome people must live there—it looked like an amazing place to live.

And soon enough, he moved there himself. But Jack wanted to see if he somehow could speed up the process of achieving it. So he decided to run a test. The first part of the test involved visiting high-end stores. Even though the prices of the goods were inaccessible at the moment, Jack acted like he owned the store the moment he stepped in. He really stepped into his role. He would try on Italian shoes and expensive suits and check out designer apparel, along with four-figure watches and jewelry.

At first, this was most uncomfortable for Jack. He felt like an interloper and as though the staff members at the stores were judging him. But as he continued this practice, he gained more confidence.

Jack often would take his friends with him on these trips. One day, one of his friends told him, "You're never going to buy anything. You are just window shopping and wasting your time." But right at that moment, Jack came across a pair of shoes that he really liked and they were on sale. Even then they were six times more expensive than any shoes he ever owned before. His mind was freaking out, but he decided to jump on it, despite the discomfort and the voice of reason in his head shouting, "Don't do it!" Soon after, he found himself a nice tailor who made him a high quality suit. He transformed from a boy in tennis shoes, printed t-shirt, and jeans to a full-grown man. From that moment on, he really began to feel like he belonged in that universe, the rich universe. After that day, no matter which store he visited, he really felt it. The store employees would give him business cards and tried to stay in contact with him. He was treated like royalty. He dressed in the finest Italian shoes and a fine suit. His appearance would demand respect and admiration everywhere he went. Not too flashy, but just appropriate for a man of his age. As his profession was realtor, he started to attract wealthier customers who were interested in higher priced homes. He just radiated confidence and trustworthiness.

Seems odd . . . or does it? Soon thereafter, Jack started to make more money than ever before. He was able to afford all those things that he was just checking out during all these months.

Encouraged by these results, Jack wondered where he could take it next—and he decided to start test-driving high-end cars. He introduced himself to sales agents and started coming so often that everybody in the dealership knew him by name. Two things that women and salesmen check on a man are his shoes and his watch. (If it's a woman, then it's the purse and shoes.) So the sales people took him pretty seriously. He even took some pictures of his favorite car and eyed them admiringly each day, and made it the screensaver image on his phone.

One day, Jack's dad saw the picture of the car on the phone and asked him about it. After Jack explained, his dad asked him, "Where are you going to put this new car, Jack? Your old car is still taking up space in your garage, no?"

So Jack decided to get rid of his current car, creating an empty space in the garage to be filled. Sure enough, the very next day he got a call from the dealership with an amazing offer he simply could not refuse. The dealership had to get rid of inventory and Jack got his dream car—with all the bells and whistles—for a great price. That added even more value in the perception of his customers. This brought more business, and that converted into more money for Jack. Even women began to be more attracted to Jack.

What Jack did was *get comfortable* with the idea of upgrading. It seemed out of reach at first, but he cultivated familiarity with it, demystifying the sense of better quality and higher standards and imbuing in his subconscious the notion that he, too, deserved and could have such things. In other words, he internalized a "wealth attitude"—knowing that rich people feel comfortable around great quality and usually, accordingly higher priced things.

Instead of saying, as most people, do, "Once I have enough money or better job, then I'll . . ." act like you *already own it.* The universe then has no choice but to treat you as if you're already that person and deliver it to you. Don't just *act about* it; *become* it. Don't just pretend to be wealthy and successful, breathe success and wealth within yourself outwards. Be happy about it and then you will have it. It's less *what* you do and more how you *feel* about it.

Start behaving like you're already rich. Create your own reality. Dress like you own the bank, not like you need a loan from it. How can one demand excellence from others if they are not projecting qualities of excellence themself? How can someone demand favors from the Universe if they are not favorable to themself, and being kind and understanding to others? How can one ask the Universe and other people to treat them better than they treat themself? God wants you to prosper, to shine, to excel. You are made in His image and you have a responsibility to represent God in the best light.

So turn it around. Start from the top and go all the way to the bottom. Feel like you are already there. Your subconscious cannot distinguish what's imaginary from what is reality. It just accepts what is served to it and accordingly complies to it.

Turn it the other way around. You should not wait to become wealthy to feel wealthy, you should feel it first and then you'll start attracting it.

If you audition for a role in a movie, you have to play the part convincingly. You have to *be* it, not just pretend. That's the secret behind all successful actors: they don't merely *act*, they *live* the role. Demi Moore went to a military boot camp before her role in *G.I. Jane*. When Richard Gere was preparing for the role of the homeless man in *Time Out of Mind*, he actually spent time with homeless people and lived with them for a while. Not to mention the dramatic physical transformations of some actors for their roles. That's why their roles are so convincing and their movies are so great. An excellent actor does not merely *interpret* their role; they truly *become* their role.

What you say to others doesn't matter nearly as much as what you keep repeating to yourself. You are the one who has to be convinced of your role. Not everyone else. Once your subconscious is convinced that you are rich, it will take every means possible to prove it to you that it is so. And you really have to master it. Work with what you have to get into the role. Smell it, feel it. How does it feel to be rich, appreciated? Actors do everything in their power to get us involved in their stories. In the same way, you need to get comfortable around wealthy situations, people, and money. This is your movie, and you should start living it on your terms.

How does it feel to be royalty? Do royals use profanity? Do they park their limousine themselves or use the valet? Paying attention to details can go a long way, since small changes can lead to big things.

You have to ask yourself: Are you acting this way for the sake of money or for the lifestyle and freedom that money provides for you?

As I said in the first chapter of this book, you already know how to make money. You can pat yourself on the back for this and say, "Well done." Because if you just made a million, wouldn't that be the very thing to do? Pour a glass of good wine or even champagne and enjoy the moment, like you just made another million. Do this every day. Actively live the role, and the rest of the movie might just fall into place.

Gratitude

I've heard countless times that the key to success is gratitude. For years, I kept a gratitude journal. I would write down a few things that I was grateful for that day and a few things that I would be grateful for manifesting the next day. However, it wasn't until I let go of expectations that the breakthrough came. I realized that gratitude really means to let go, to trust the process and the Universe. Of course, you should work towards your goal; but let the Universe be in command of the style of delivery. That made a huge difference for me.

You have to feel it first. You have to make yourself feel that sensation, to have infinite trust in the process.

When you feel grateful, it's hard to feel anxiety, depression, stress, or worry—because those feelings are the exact opposite of gratitude. We are not machines; we cannot just command ourselves to feel a certain way. However, we can take certain steps that move us from a more negative state of mind to a more grateful one. Remember: your "inner treasure chest" is determined by your stress level. So the lower your stress is, the greater that treasure chest has the potential to become.

This doesn't mean having blind faith and risking everything. However, there are some big steps that you can take consistently to cross from negative emotions to a state of grace.

It's important to clarify that showing and feeling gratitude does not mean merely saying thank you. It means really *feeling* a certain way with your whole body, mind, and spirit. You can feel "grateful" for the $100 that you earned today while also being irritated that you are a few dollars short for something you would like to buy. Instead, you should be grateful for the $100 and have faith that the extra few dollars you need will come your way at the appropriate time. The first scenario can't be an attitude of gratitude, because you're complaining. The second one is real gratitude that opens your channels to even more blessings.

It is easy to feel gratitude once when you understand that the challenges the Universe has thrown at you are actually opportunities to grow. Remember the story about Eric in the chapter "The Magician". The Universe put him through the challenge. He became very scared and it looked like a disaster to him, but it turned out to be a great win. What situations can you remember in your life when you felt that it's a disaster, but it turned out to be a blessing? By my experience, the bigger the challenge, the bigger the blessings. Challenges are like a boot camp. They are preparing you for what the Universe is about to deliver for you. When God is about to grant your wish, He does not just throw it in front of you, He puts you in position and gives you a chance to go get it. Because whatever you asked for, it's a bigger responsibility than what you had before; therefore, the Universe has to make sure that you're up to the challenge, that you're not about to quit at the first little obstacle. The Universe has to make sure that you are committed before investing in you. If your wish was to start your own business, the Universe has to be convinced that you can take care of the increased workload and the people who are going to depend on your corporation. That's why you have to go through tests. When you demonstrate that you are committed to pursuing a goal, when you don't stress and you don't back out, you show that you have grown and that it is time to move forward. Consider it a contract with the Universe. The Universe provides—but you have to live up to your end of the bargain. Embrace challenges because challenges are a sign that the Universe is granting your wish.

Gratitude isn't just a sentence or a statement; it's your entire attitude and your emotions. There is no way that you can feel gratitude if you are upset or stressed. When you own your feelings, that's the true moment of gratitude. That's when your gratitude is genuine. It's when you pay attention to the other person, instead of "being in your head" and thinking about yourself all the time.

The Universe is always working in your favor whether you see it that way or not. One day, I saw this little kitty with her head stuck in a glass jar. Two guys were trying to get her out. One of them picked up a hammer, and as they tried carefully to break the glass just enough to free the kitten, the kitten resisted and thrashed about in a panic. The poor thing must have been petrified, and the guys were having a hard time to keep her still. Finally, with a precise and controlled strike of the hammer, they broke the jar and the kitten was saved, unharmed. But the kitten did not make it easy for them—because she didn't trust them. She was resisting.

I wonder how often we react the same way towards the Universe. Often we freak out in tough situations and, like the kitten, lash out against the Universe. We twitch and turn and resist. But as we do so, we are working against ourselves by keeping the Universe from helping us.

Think of your rainy days as a transition period—a time when the rain helps the seeds that you've planted grow. Stay the course; stick around through the rain. Eventually, the seeds will grow and bear fruit.

Being out in the spotlight involves certain risks. If you asked for something that you really want to happen, your guardian—a.k.a. Subconscious Mind—has to build you up first so that you can be up to the challenge. When you make a million dollars, you have a million responsibilities; when you make a billion dollars, you have a billion responsibilities. Most people need training on taking care of a million responsibilities. The ones who persist are the ones who are rewarded.

When we ask the Universe for blessings, those blessings sometimes come disguised as hardships or setbacks. They are not truly setbacks, but setups.

In the early 1980's, Mark was just another young man on his daily grind. He was sharing a three-bedroom apartment with another five people and he worked for a PC software company. He was fired less than a year later for meeting with a client to procure new business instead of opening the store. That event convinced him to become an entrepreneur and start his own company. Today, Mark Cuban's net-worth is over 3 billion dollars and he owns an NBA team in addition to many successful companies. What looked like a setback was actually a push forward. The Universe knows exactly how to work on you. When you ask the Universe for something, the Universe does not just deliver it to you, it gives you the opportunity for you to go find it yourself.

It's just the wrapping that the package is delivered in. A dog that barks at the mailman when the mailman is carrying a pack of treats ordered by the dog's owner will scare away the mailman and won't get his treats. Don't despair or get discouraged by what might look like a setback. It's just a method of delivery for blessings that you asked for.

Being Happy Now

An often bandied-about quote (sometimes erroneously attributed to Siddhartha Gautama, a.k.a. the Buddha) says, "There is no path to happiness. Happiness is the path." Most people think, "One day when I have enough money, I can relax and then I will be happy." The truth is it works the other way around. If you can be relaxed and happy now, you will attract the money and the lifestyle you want.

Let's say your goal is $1,000. Once you reach that goal, it shifts to $10,000, after that $100,000, and so on. But if you have a persistently bad mood and negative outlook, it will almost certainly drag you back to the beginning. Your mood should not *depend* on your circumstances; rather, your mood has the power to *change* your circumstances.

Remember: your subconscious is always looking to protect you. So if money frustrates you, it has to keep that source of frustration away from you. If you remain relaxed and happy, there is no reason why you would not get almost anything you ask for. If you are a little baby and the toys that your parents give you make you upset, don't you think that your parents will begin to take things away from you until they realize what made you cry? They don't want you upset. In the same way, the Universe is going to take things from you; it does not want you upset.

The Universe is trying to get through to you all the time. All you have to do is calm down and listen. Meditate. Enjoy some relaxation and stand still at your special place. You must have that intimacy with yourself in order to figure out who you are.

HOW TO GET MONEY

Chapter Eleven:
The Master Key

The Master Key

Alright dear reader, it's time to reveal the Master Key. The Master Key can be summed up in one word only. It's the key that is behind virtually any sustainable success achieved on this planet. It's the word that describes how Tomas Edison found the right material to create the first sustainable light bulb. It's the word that describes how our forefathers founded the United States of America despite the fact that by signing the Declaration of Independence, they put their lives on the line. It's the word that describes how Edmund Hillary and Tenzing Norgay were the first ones to scale the top of Mount Everest. It's the word that describes how the Wright Brothers managed to take off in an airplane and fly. It's the word that describes how Mahatma Gandhi managed to lead India to independence from British rule of India. It's the word that describes how Nelson Mandela overcame 27 years of prison and became the first black head of state and the first elected in a fully representative election as President of South Africa. It's the word that describes how Muhammad Ali became such a successful athlete, icon, and example of racial pride for African Americans and resistance to white domination during the Civil Rights Movement in the United States of America. It was described through words such as persistence, sustainability, and perseverance. And that is close enough, but being persistent does not have the depth and dimension to it. It sounds more like push it until it breaks. What if it doesn't break right away?

It does not let you have excuses, it does not give you quitting as an option, it helps you remain on track, and it inspires you to figure things out along the way.

It takes a commitment when you work day and night and there are no results to show for all your effort . . . yet! It takes commitment to believe in yourself when everybody else thinks you are foolish for putting your time and effort into something that might not work. Just as it takes commitment to stay in a marriage, it also takes commitment to carry your goal through to its completion.

And that word is "commitment". Yes my dear reader, <u>commitment is the Master Key</u>.

Most people acknowledge that commitment is critical to success—and not just in business. After all, how does a marriage work? Because both people involved have made a commitment to each other. If one person goes into a marriage with one foot in and one foot out, it's not going to work. People in relationships should ask, "What can I give? How can I contribute? What can we do to make this work?" rather than, "What's in this for me? What do *I* get?" You can apply the same logic to any personal or professional undertaking. If you aren't committed to it, it's probably doomed to failure.

Of course, commitment requires patience—and that can be a tall order for anyone. Most people are looking to make a quick buck. But the approach that will offer the most benefit in the long run will take time. A lot of small changes over a period of time are what make all the difference—not one big change, but slowly emerging, building, developing. Don't seek a major transformation overnight; focus on one small change at a time. In his book *Outliers,* author

Malcolm Gladwell posits that to master any craft, a person has to spend on average 10,000 hours practicing it. If you would spend that much time in a single craft or a skill, what do you think would happen?

Consider this hypothetical scenario. Joe set his goal and started off towards it, determined, without looking back. He decided to become a barber. So after he took a crash course and found a salon, he started his new craft. It was going well for the first week, but then it became slow. Joe could barely cover his living expenses. One day, a customer walked in and said that there is great money in being a massage therapist. Joe decided to take that route. So he took another crash course, found a salon, and started that job. But the same scenario occurred. After a few weeks of decent work, it slowed down again. One day, a customer came through who, after hearing Joe's complaining, advised him to try a valet parking job. That's where the big money is.

At the same time, Brian started working for a flood restoration company. His money was not going far at that moment either, but Brian decided to educate himself and to learn more about restoration and fixing homes, so he was promoted and was given a raise. He was providing better service to his clients and to his company, so he was rewarded. One day, in the middle of the economic crash, Brian decided that he wants to retire by the age of 45, so he told his boss that he would like to open his own company—and he did! All his friends and relatives advised Brian not to do such a "foolish" thing. Their argument was that the economy is down and that he already had a secure job, which paid him well. Brian did not budge and left to pursue his goal. At the beginning, he really endured some very difficult days, sitting in his truck, his office at the time, and was not receiving a single call. He had days when he had his last dollar in his pocket and that was all he could spend for food that day. But as he pursued and worked at upgrading his skills, knowledge, and services to his clients, things started to turn for the better. Brian gave supreme, top-notch service and he had high-end clients. He connected more with the local community and always looked at how he could improve his business and also things around him. Fast forward to today: earlier this year, Brian purchased an entire building in the city of Los Angeles, CA. Brian is today a multi-millionaire at 45 years of age.

Joe wanted quick results and was zigzagging through life. He was never interested in mastering anything. He liked to party a lot and hang out with friends on a daily basis. When Joe started his first job, he was after a quick buck. He did not care much about it. He did not even like his boss, the job, or the customers. It didn't work out as quickly for him as Joe had imagined it would; so he decided to change his goal to a much easier one this time. He had seen a shinier object on the horizon and took off for it.

But that didn't work out either, so he set another goal. In the meantime, after he set his first goal, the Universe began to respond, but since Joe had changed course, the Universe had to abort the first goal. Then, the Universe did the same with the second goal—but once again, it was forced to abandon it because Joe himself had abandoned that goal.

At the same time, Brian was committed to his job, and afterwards to his own business. Yes, there were some days when he felt discouraged, but he never quit and kept developing himself and his service, always keeping in mind his goal to retire by age 45. Brian said that once he got some money as a cushion, the jobs started to pour in themselves.

People often see successful people and assume that their success happened overnight. They don't see the years of commitment, dedication, persistence, and perseverance that preceded it. And overnight success can vanish as quickly as it happens. Remember, your subconscious is here to keep you "safe," even to your own detriment.

What situations in your life can you remember when you were after something that did not work out, but soon after, you got exactly what you wanted, just better?

Path To Success Illustration

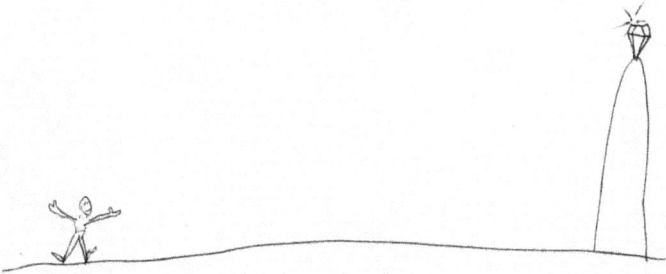

Let's take person "A".

Person "A" sees what he would like to achieve and sets a goal. Let the diamond on the top of the hill represent that goal.

Then person "A" starts working towards the goal. He starts to build a ramp to reach high towards the hill and grab the prize. The process is too slow for person "A" so he decides to cut some corners and try a different approach. Person "A" does not have a plan nor discipline so now tries piling things up underneath the hill in order to climb on it and move up towards the prize.

Person "A" is distracted easily by the latest gossip, reality shows, games, and other diversions. He likes to party and can't stand spending time working.

He tries a different approach once more by laying bricks.

Finally, he gives it one more desperate attempt but soon enough quits.

Now let's take Person "B".

Person "B" sees what he would like to achieve and sets a goal. The diamond on the top of the hill represents that goal.

Person "B" finds a pile of wood and starts building a ramp in order to climb up and grab the goal.

It turned out that wood alone wouldn't be strong enough for him to reach his goal. So person "B" does research and looks for a solution. He gets educated.

He brings bricks and continues to build a sturdier ramp. As it reaches a certain point, not even bricks are able to withhold his weight. Part of the ramp crumbles. So person "B" is paying attention and looks for guidance, in other words "thinks".

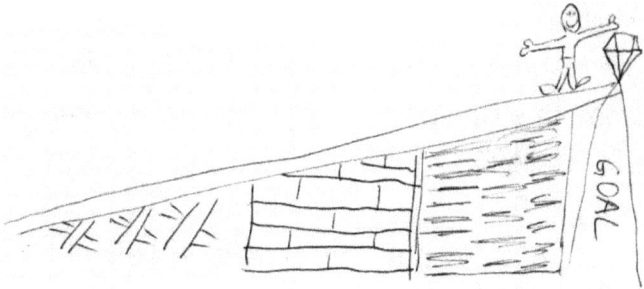

He comes to a realization after recalling that the tallest buildings are built with a mixture of concrete and steel bars. So, person "B" uses those materials and finally finishes the ramp, then picks up the   prize!

Now here is the really important outcome. Once the ramp is built, person "B" has easy access each time a new opportunity (diamond) appears. That is how commitment works and why you make money based on your value. This ramp can represent ten or more years of schooling for a person to become a doctor, an architect, or any other craft you want to master with or without formal education. When you are an architect, you can build in any country on virtually any continent. You mastered it. If you were selling cars for ten years, paid attention, and learned the craft, surely you would open your own dealership by that time. But if you were just selling during your working hours and playing video games and partying the rest of the time, you would end up like person "A" from this illustration, a person who complains how life is not fair and hates their job. In other words, if you pay first . . .

But even if you master a skill but you stop upgrading, your ramp will deteriorate. You have to learn all the time. Listen and pay attention.

You Can Have Almost Anything You Want If . . .

You can have almost anything you want if you are willing to pay the price—and most of the time, that price is commitment. Successful people do what's necessary and often uncomfortable, while others do what is convenient.

You can have a great body if you commit to doing certain things, like working out regularly and maintaining a certain diet. This also means committing to doing the research. No two human beings are the same; something that works for one person might not work for someone else. And in most cases that is not enough. People with killer looks don't go on a diet for a month and then expect the results to stick; it's a long-term and probably lifetime effort. That's why some people are running in circles when it comes to getting in shape. They have a goal, they do an exercise regime for a month, and then after they reach their goal, they revert to eating unhealthy food and living a sedentary lifestyle. Some people quit before they even see results. If you are serious about it, you need to commit. Having a healthy body is a *lifestyle*, not a two-month-long project. If you think that you cannot survive on eating salads, you have to figure out what kind of food you can commit to for the rest of your life in order to get what you are looking for. Success is a lifestyle, not a project.

How does someone find (and keep) their life partner? Through commitment, and deciding that this is a priority. Maybe this means figuring out how to earn a little more so you can be a good provider, or taking better care of your appearance. Perhaps you need to develop your intellect, or cultivate qualities that might attract another person.

Likewise, when you decide to whom it is that you are going to commit, you must be sure that that person possesses most of the qualities that *you* are looking for. It has to be someone with whom you can imagine spending the rest of your life. No one is ever a 100% match; but if you can find someone who meets the majority of your ideals, you can grow together. If you try to find the "perfect" match, guess what? That person does not need you—because all you are looking for is to be taken care of. There's nothing wrong with being taken care of, but you need to give something in return. If you want a serious relationship, you can't just "give it a try," you must *commit.*

What is the path to riches? By promising yourself that this is a priority, and by determining what you need to do to get there. You have to be willing to do whatever it takes. Not what feels comfortable, but whatever is necessary. As long as these actions don't violate other people's lives, resources, nature, or divine and earthly laws, you can make that promise to yourself. You have to become that. You cannot "fake it till you make it", if you are doing that to convince other people. It's not about you demonstrating to others. It's between you and yourself. There is not a matter of just trying. Only commitment. And by making that kind of commitment, you will find the means and resources to reach it. You have to commit most of your time and energy until you succeed. No one ever got rich by distracting themself with gossip, reality shows, or drama on TV or the Internet, unless it's that person's profession. No one got rich following other people on social media. When you pay attention to others, you bring them money. But if you want to make money, you have to bring your focus back to you. There are a lot of distractions around us nowadays—so much information that we have a hard time distinguishing what is what. And as long as your mind is distracted by these things, there won't be space left for things of value to you.

There is no *absolute* truth; you hold your own truth, and that depends on the angle from which you are looking. You need to research and search for yourself within yourself to find out what works for you.

However, there are some universal laws that serve as the rules of the game. The better you know the rules, the better you can understand and gain greater results—and achieve your goals.

Riches sometimes come in streams, sometimes in waves. The deeper the sink, the higher the wave, but you have to be prepared by feeling good about it first.

The Success Ladder

1. You have to do what <u>it</u> takes, not what feels comfortable.
2. Things that you are not used to usually feel pretty uncomfortable at first.
3. Once you get used to these things, they become more comfortable.
4. Repetition is what transforms uncomfortable to comfortable.

Chapter Twelve: Contribution

The Ten Percent

If you can't believe that others deserve their money, how could you be sure that you deserve it yourself? What are your feelings towards rich and successful people? What are your feelings towards money in general? Remember: your feelings dictate your results.

In 2016, it was estimated that 10% of the population holds 76% of all the money on this planet. How does that make you feel? Do you think that this is unjust? Do you think that the ones who have more should pay more?

We've already discussed how money finds its way to the people who attract it best. I would bet that if you distributed money from each member of that

10%, that wealth would find its way back to them in pretty short time. The Universe needs it's Jeff Bezoses and its Richard Bransons to bring blessings and make everyone else's lives easier with their inventions and ideas.

How many people can serve one person if it is up to their physical presence and serving one by one? If I would write this book by hand, one by one for each customer, how many customers could I serve at once? But if I print this book, I can reach far more people with a single stroke. If you are a hairdresser, how many people can you serve at once? Now if you own a hair salon and hire a few people to work for you, you can serve more people at the same time. And if we go even further and you create a brand from it and franchise it, how many people does that enable you to serve now? Now let's be reminded how many people Mark Zuckerberg and Bill Gates serve. How many PC's are there in the world again, how many people use Facebook? That's wherein lie their riches. They serve more people than anyone else in the field, with very little effort. The more you serve, the more you get. I came to the conclusion that if our primary purpose is to prosper and to multiply, as the Bible says, then our main purpose is to serve and to create.

If you walk down a busy street on an average day, three out of a hundred people who pass you by belong to the top 10%. Every tenth person you see is wealthy. All of a sudden, when you change your perspective, that sounds somehow good, doesn't it? You are surrounded by wealth.

The efficiency of an army depends on a hierarchy divided by rank. If everyone was a general, there would be chaos. The same applies to wealth and the socioeconomic division of society. If there were no rank, leaders would appear eventually and start to bring order to the chaos.

Now here is the great news: you can become a leader too. Nothing comes for free; but with dedication—or better yet, commitment—you can acquire the necessary education and training to become a leader just as you can ascend to wealth.

The Internet provides amazing opportunities that enable you to accomplish a lot by investing very little. Much has changed in even just a few generations. In the past, in order to have a store, an entrepreneur had to have a building and a warehouse and find goods from somewhere. Today, you have a chance to make money from home without the burdens of brick-and-mortar commerce. How amazing is that?

Your opportunity is here and now. We literally are living during the best time in human history to start and to run our own business, and to have control of our own destiny. Digital books, music, blogs, and videos abound. It is mind-blowing how many things can be done online. You can package and sell your knowledge online through webinars, online training, coaching, consulting, and the like. You can put your idea out into the world and raise money to make your vision a reality through crowd funding platforms like Kickstarter, Indiegogo, GoFundMe, to name a few. You can sell a physical product and start your ecommerce business to almost anyone on the planet through sites like Amazon, BigCommerce, Shopify, to name a few. You can create your website very easily with the help of Squarespace, Wix, and Godaddy, to name a few. You can hire freelancers to do work for you for five dollars already at Fiverr or Upwork and many others. You can share your ideas, build an audience, and tap into your personal creativity to build a passionate, loyal fan base through social media, blogging, YouTube, and others. AND, you can get paid from anywhere in the world instantly with websites and apps like PayPal, Stripe, and Venmo. You can learn how to do things through YouTube videos and tutorials, like how to put your website together and how to promote it. You can even get suggestions as to what online business is worthy for you to start. All this is available to you from no cost at all to a very little upfront expense. The Internet Age provides unprecedented opportunities for making money. You just have to act on them.

The Richest Ones

We've already discussed how time is more valuable than money—and how our time here is limited, but money is not. When you begin a pursuit in business, you probably have more time than money. In the beginning, you have to invest a lot of time into crafting a necessary skill set. You must practice dedication and commitment. As you invest your time in developing certain skills, you become more valuable on the market.

However, it's important to remain aware that skills that are highly valuable or marketable now *may not be so in the future.* Therefore, learning new skills—keeping up with the times, improving, and upgrading—is critical. One must stay relevant on the market.

What are the most profitable skill sets a person might have? Well, those who serve the greatest number of people tend to be the wealthiest. One such individual is Bill Gates, an American business magnate and co-founder of Microsoft. How did he get to where he is? What was his path, or formula for success? For Gates, the formula was to provide to the greatest number of people possible a valuable product or service, while spending the least amount of time and energy.

Average people accept jobs that barely enable them to take care of themselves and their family. Wealthy people create jobs that take care of others and *their* families. Average people often adopt the mindset that someone else should take care of them. But helping *others* find a way to make money is a surefire way of enriching yourself. Bill Gates exemplifies this principle in action; his product, *Microsoft Windows*, helps others to communicate, do work, have fun, and more. And on top of that, relatively little energy is spent on its production. Once it is built, it can be distributed digitally. So if you can find a way to serve as many people as possible with the least energy spent, that's ideal.

That's what the most productive business owners do. If you own just one restaurant, you can employ a limited number of people. But what if you were to outsource and build up an international brand, a chain of stores, or a franchise?

Money is a form of energy that I can pass on to others and gain even greater results. In agriculture, you need to keep a part of your seeds to plant; and in business, you need to seed your money wisely.

Consider Warren Buffet, American business magnate and investor. His investing helps create jobs. He takes an average company, reshapes it, and makes

172

it highly profitable. Mexican billionaire Carlos Slim owns a telecommunication company. How many people own telephones and smart phones and rely on that technology day to day? Can you comprehend the number of people those mentioned Billionaires serve. Well, that's the reason they were so handsomely rewarded.

This doesn't just exist in the world of business. A musician brings joy and influences people's emotions. Now, if a musician could only perform for people in the same room that they were in, their reach would be limited. But thanks to today's technology, a digital copy of a musician's record is available for everyone at the same time. Not just sound, but video and photos too. Again, with a small investment of time and energy, that musician can reach a wide audience.

We should ask ourselves: Is there a way I could multiple my talent or skills in such a way? Can my talent or skill set provide a genuine service that is needed?

Pay First: Play Later

There is a price for everything in life, and not necessarily a monetary one. The difference is that rich people pay it forward. They know that there are no free rides. Everything that you think you got for free was actually, in one way or another, bought on credit, and the longer you wait, the more interest is going to be charged to you.

Take, for example, a car. Often, people buy cheap cars because they think they're saving money that way. Rich people buy reliable, higher quality cars that may seem pricey, but that last longer and have the "extras" built in which cost other people more.

Mass-produced, highly processed food cannot be healthy. To keep such food sanitary and preserve it for transportation over long distances, it has to be processed with a lot of chemicals. Cheaper, unhealthy food has a steep cost paid by your physical well-being (in addition to the price of doctors you have to visit).

Rich people buy insurance; others don't. A dollar in the right place today is 100 dollars gained in the future; a dollar in the wrong place today is 100 dollars of debt down the road. These are the ways that the rich pay first and play later, while other people play first and pay later.

The same applies to labor and how you use your time. Work now and reap the benefits later, rather than succumbing to instant gratification and suffering tomorrow for your lack of initiative today.

There's a story about the grasshopper and the ant. The entire summer, while the ant was gathering food, the grasshopper was singing lazily and mocking the ant. When winter came, the hungry grasshopper begged the ant to spare some food. "What did you do the whole summer?" asked the ant. "I was singing," replied the grasshopper. "Well, then you can dance the winter away," said the ant. The ant represents the 10% who prepare themselves and grasshopper represents the other 90% who just look how to be entertained.

I know this doctor, a friend of mine who comes from Togo in Africa. He get's the most respect wherever he goes. He came to the United States to study medicine about seventeen years ago. He told me that he came with $300 in his pocket and built his way through education. He had so many setbacks and challenges, but he stayed committed all the way for some 15 years. That's how long it took him to finish his degree. After he finished his education, being the best in his field, he could choose where to work and he decided to stay in the United States. You see, a person with that level of education is very highly paid, very much respected, and can choose any place in the world to live, because of a high demand. His education paid off well. You see, he paid it first, now he can play. He can choose to go back to Togo, Europe, Asia, the Americas, Australia, or anywhere in the world. He is very respected, well rewarded (paid), and welcomed everywhere. Now compare him to Joe from the chapter "The Ultimate Secret of Success".

The Bank

Meet Pete. Pete was one of those people who always thought that he deserved more but had to settle for less until his "day would come." He prayed to God every day to bless him abundantly and send him money to solve all his life's problems. And every week, Pete played the lottery. Then one day, after many years of trying, his numbers were pulled. Pete became a lottery winner. He won a cool two million dollars. It was *finally* his moment, his time.

That was a few years back. Today, Pete is in debt. How is that possible? Well, since Pete was not used to having money, he did not know how to keep it. He spent it in all the wrong places. Pete wanted so much to be validated and to show how good a person he was that he started buying new cars for his friends and peers and helping his family. Instead of gratitude, they pressured Pete so much that he couldn't stand it anymore. Pete became so desperate that he prayed to God to take the money away from him.

The money never truly belonged to Pete. He was just a distribution channel.

When the Universe gives you money, it's because the Universe trusts you to use or distribute it well. We are merely a distribution center for the

Universe—almost a bank. And the better job we do, the more engagement we receive from the Universe.

Now if you were a central bank, would you distribute money through someone who says money is the root of all evil? Or through someone who spends their money to please all their friends and seeks to buy validation through conspicuous consumption? Would you give it to a person who breaks down or gets irritated at every little challenge and complains most of the time?

The Universe does not put in front of us anything that we are unable to handle. But we often become so scared and intimidated that we have to get rid of it—and fast! Just like Pete did.

You don't necessarily receive what you *ask* the Universe to give you or what you need; rather, you get the amount of money that you feel comfortable with. Everything beyond that is taken from you. When the Universe is confident that you can overcome certain challenges, you earn its trust.

Are you giving people an opportunity to receive their own blessings and enable them? Or are you trying to buy their sympathy and validation? Are you creating jobs or giving money just to be accepted?

When the Universe enriches someone, it wants them to use it on themself in a way that it helps others. Otherwise it will be passed on to a person who knows how to distribute it well.

The money that we have is not ours; it never has been. We cannot take it to the grave with us. The Universe trusts us to be great bankers, to invest wisely. Ideally, we can create opportunities and assist other people to improve their lives and make money. We also have to have compassion and help those who can't help themselves, too. There is nothing wrong with giving some to charity, to your local church, and to those who are unable to help themselves; but the best use is to enable people to help themselves.

Most rich people invest their money in a way that bears fruit. This helps to speed up the financial ecosystem, which in turn benefits *more* people—and that's the exact reason why the Universe trusts these people initially. They are the ones who can engender expansion and growth.

The Roman Empire lasted for over five hundred years. One of the main reasons that it was so prosperous and long-lasting was that the leaders were not just taking from conquered nations; they were giving value back as well. They built roads, infrastructure, and libraries. They allowed some measure of localized governance. They balanced out well their rule with people's autonomy. Generally, they actually improved people's lives in conquered territories and brought many blessings. Many other conquerors during history did not last so long for the simple fact that they were just taking—and you can't just take. You have to give a part back to support the eco-system. It's impossible to have a harvest next year if you did not invest a part of the seeds from this season to use in the next one.

You can feel good about giving, because it's so much more than just handing out money; it's giving others the opportunity to make their own. And the more you do, with less energy or time spent, the better off you are. That's the ultimate wealth eco-system. Do you see yourself as a giver or taker? Do you invest in advertising, do you hire other people to do jobs for you, do you donate? You see, not all the money is for you to keep. The more you seed, the more you sow. That's how you support the eco-system, the economy, jobs, and eventually it comes back to you.

Being rich is not so much about keeping the money as it is about *seeding* the money. Over divine purpose on this planet is to serve and to create. The people who are most valued are those who serve the most.

Seeding money means that we are putting it back into the economy, paying our taxes, supporting our places of worship, and other causes, places, people, and events we find worthy—and paying ourselves to save money. Rich people just know better where the fertile soil is to seed their money. Wealthy people create things of value that give opportunity to others and money to themselves.

Chapter Thirteen: Creativity

Edison Vs. Tesla

"I have not failed. I've just found 10,000 ways that won't work." - Thomas Edison

"Be alone; that is the secret of invention. Be alone; that is when ideas are born." - Nikola Tesla

Thomas Edison and Nikola Tesla are without a doubt two of the greatest inventors of the 19th century. They were also scientific and entrepreneurial rivals in their time; and their respective approaches were rather different. While Edison pushed and persisted, Tesla was more meditative—creating more in alignment with the Universe. Both approaches can produce results; but I favor Tesla's method. For one

HOW TO GET MONEY

thing, Nikola is my countryman. We both were born in Croatia and moved to the United States.

For another, I admire this viewpoint from Tesla, who once said, "My brain is only a receiver. In the Universe there is a core from which we obtain knowledge, strength, and inspiration. I have not penetrated into the secrets of this core, but I know that it exists." In contrast, Edison said, "Our greatest weakness lies in giving up. The most certain way to succeed is always to try just one more time." At the same time, Edison's advice highlights the importance of commitment—while Tesla highlights the importance of getting connected to the Universe. And both are equally important.

Just imagine the world today if those two brilliant people could have put their differences aside and worked together?

Creativity

A long time ago, when MySpace was the dominant social network website, I had an idea to create a business portal for business professionals and businesses. I actually even created the website and had a few friends of mine, business owners, create their profiles there. Soon after, I lost interest in it and let it go. A few years later, LinkedIn started to create some noise and gain popularity. The LinkedIn site has an Alexa Internet ranking as the 20th most popular website in the world. In 2016, Microsoft acquired LinkedIn for approximately $26.4 billion.

We've all had an experience when someone comes up with a great idea and then that same idea materializes later thanks to someone else, and we say, "Hey, I had exactly the same idea about a year ago! I would have all those millions myself if I had acted on it!"

So why *didn't* you act upon it?

As I said throughout this book, our purpose on this planet is to contribute to improving the quality of our lives here; in short, to support, to create, and to participate in development. So where are those ideas generated? They come out of the blue, right?

Yes, because that's what the Universe is communicating to us. An idea is a message from the

Universe. We get that message because the Universe is looking to recruit someone to give birth to an idea—specifically, something that will help stimulate our growth. If we don't act on it, the Universe passes the idea on to another person, and if necessary another and another, until someone finally acts on it and brings the idea to life.

So what happens if you actually decide to act on this idea? Imagine that the Universe is your right foot and your action is your left foot. The Universe made its first step and passed you on an idea. Now if you act on it, that means you take a step with your left foot. Now you are walking, things are in motion. Then, I believe the Universe takes another step, propelling you forward, helping you get things off the ground.

Sometimes you come to a wall, a setback that is difficult to overcome. That's where most people decide not to take further steps. If they only knew that there are doors in that wall. It takes effort to look at things from a different perspective in order to find those doors.

Once you find them, you need a password to unlock them. That password is CREATIVITY—and the motor of creativity is imagination. Imagination and creativity are not limited to artists. A great merchant uses their imagination to figure out how to serve clients the best way possible. A great cook uses their imagination to come up with new specialties. A great engineer designs marvelous structures in an innovative way.

The more and better we create, the more we are rewarded—whether we're creating something totally new or improving an existing thing.

Therefore, by communicating to the Universe, you keep walking forward and our creativity is awakened. If your progress stalls, the best option that I know is to stop for a minute, try to look at things from a different perspective, and through your inner self communicate with the Universe using meditation or some other methods that let you be with yourself and your inner voice. Your inner voice is your best friend and is connected to the eternal source, divine intelligence. If you just keep pushing, most likely you have disconnected from your inner self and messages and became distracted by things around you. That's when one foot is dragging the other. That's why the process sometimes can be slow and frustrating.

And that's exactly what happens when people try to force things and do too much too soon and with too little. A planted seed takes time and dedication to germinate and to grow.

I once knew a gentleman named Jimmy who used to own a jewelry shop. As gold prices are ever-changing, he would rely on his inner voice to help him decide when he should invest more in his inventory and when he should wait to purchase new quantities of gold. It worked so well for Jimmy that he ended up buying up most of his competitors' stores in his town for discounted prices.

Some people have it all just because . . . they would ask.

Your Pot of Gold

Let's say that someone sees another person's pot of gold at the top of the hill and starts to go after it. But the Universe put that gold there for *that* person; the person going after it has a pot of gold elsewhere. The Universe tries to tell this covetous person—in some way or another—"This is not your pot of gold." But they don't listen, and insist on climbing towards someone else's pot of gold. The Universe speaks up again, this time a little bit louder. The person still does not listen and continues up the hill. The Universe speaks again, this time screaming at the person, grabbing their hand, pulling them back. The person starts to curse at the Universe, dusts themself off, and continues once again towards that pot of gold.

The Universe has had enough by this time—and just when that person is nearing the top of the hill, drags the person down the hill away from the gold that is not meant for them. Can you imagine that person's feelings after ascending the hill and coming nearly within arm's reach of the pot of gold they desired so strongly? It seemed so easy, yet it did not work.

Often, what appears easily accessible—just a short climb up the hill—is actually the result of someone else's years of labor, commitment, and sacrifice. Let others have their pots of gold; you have to find your own. The guy that advised Joe that there is great money in valet parking was making a killing there, but it did not work for Joe.

Success follows you when you walk with purpose, commitment, and faith, not when you're zigzagging through life. I said that success follows. That's because you have to give it time to catch up to you, but if you are changing your path all the time, you're just resetting your chances back to zero each time.

What situations in your life can you remember when you were after something that did not work out, but soon after you got exactly the same thing, only better?

Start listening to your inner voice. That's how you will discover your own purpose and your own pot of gold, which no one will be able to take away from you.

Your Million-Dollar Idea

At one of my church meetings, I met Anthony. Anthony told us his life story. At one point in his life he was homeless. He did not know what to do so he started praying and one day the Holy Spirit spoke to him. He said: "Go wash windows". Anthony was confused at first, but then he started to wash windows. He started first washing car windows on street corners. Soon after, he got a little bit of money and he bought himself a trailer as a home. But he decided to lease it to create an income source and kept living on the streets. After he earned some more money, he bought himself a place, upgraded his clothes and appearance, and started washing people's house windows. Fast forward—today, Anthony owns over ten houses, and his window washing company, where he employs over some one hundred people, is bringing in millions of dollars of profit every year. And it all started with that voice in his head.

Everything in existence was once just an idea. Just a thought. Just an image in someone's head. Then another thought came and another one until the idea was fully conceived and realized. And the Universe has one for each of us. It communicates with us all the time—and we can do that when we just stop and listen, instead of looking for the answer outside of us.

Legend says that Nikola Tesla came up with an idea about alternating current one day by watching a sunset in a park. Nowadays, alternating current is pretty much standard for every home around the globe. It powers all of the electrical gadgets that we use. Tesla had a vision. He acted upon it and discovered how to answer the technical challenge of making a workable AC electrical system to turn a motor.

This book that you hold in your hand was at first just an idea. I was inspired and I acted on it. I dedicated myself to seeing it through to its completion. In fact, I see myself here only as a messenger. It was the Universe that injected those ideas into my mind, and I just put them on paper.

Reach out to the Universe, listen, and have patience. You too can be blessed with a million-dollar idea. Then, commit yourself, be disciplined, stay the course, and in time you will get what you set out to achieve.

Chapter Fourteen: Epilogue

How You Use The Master Key

Before you get to the Master Key, you need to bypass two guardians that go by the names "Contribution" and "Creativity". What does that mean? Well, many people commit to many things but those things don't bare the fruits they really wanted. If you commit to video games, can you make a living from it? Some people do, but most don't. What if you committed to a wrong person? You see, Contribution and Creativity help you to define your purpose, in other words, a service that you are willing to render to humanity. And creativity serves that you don't deliver something existing but rather something highly needed or improved, something of great demand on this planet.

Imagine if there is a space where all thoughts from all people on this planet meet and if there is a need for something, that message grows louder. Like, what if enough critical mass of the people thought about the need for a fully functional electric car. Now, imagine that you are Elon Musk and by isolating yourself and cancelling the outside noise, you are able to tap into that field where you get a signal of what is needed on this planet. That's how valuable ideas are born. The opposite of that is copying someone else's success, just for monetary gain. That's how you get through to your creation in order to make a contribution and you are ready to use the Master Key.

The interesting thing is that the Pyramid of Success works the other way around as well. After an idea comes to mind and inspires you, you can implement that idea in a way that can be of service. Then, you commit to making it a reality by using your creative faculties. You are granted to use the Master Key to do this in the most successful way. This approach will garner you much greater rewards than if you merely commit to someone else's idea. You can start from the top and go all the way to the bottom.

Therefore, let's start.

10. The Master Key

in other words commitment, is carried through faith and discipline. You have to believe in order to achieve and you have to move systematically towards your goal. You have to work on your goal daily and most likely for years. If it doesn't work at first, you have to find out how to make it work. Bill Gates did not take a day off until he was 30 years of age. Hip hop legend LL Cool J was rapping since the age of nine and had his first shot at success at the age of sixteen when he chased producer and record label owner Rick Rubin to sign a record deal and publish his first song. Abraham Lincoln had seven failed campaigns prior to becoming the President of the United States. Henry Ford ran three unsuccessful businesses before the age of fifty-three, when he succeeded with Ford Motors. You see, the most misused phrase—follow your passion—is not really all that. If you ask a class of students in elementary school what would they like to be when they grow up, ninety percent would like to be a TV star, singer, actor, or a football or basketball player. But do we need that many athletes and entertainers? You see, average people get impressed easily by shiny objects and they think that in order to get them, they have to do what everyone else is doing. Nothing could be further from the truth. You have to find your own path, a path to serve and to create.

9. Faith

is crucial as sometimes there is no solution on the horizon. You have to believe it first. You can identify people of faith exactly as they walk through the world with a high dose of certainty and self-confidence. They are not easy to deceive. Through faith, you display readiness to receive what you asked for. Generally, through my experience, the bigger pressure you can take, the bigger the reword is at the other end. People in faith sustain better and carry through to the end.

Everybody who ever worked in a gym is aware of the fact that muscles need to break down in order to grow. Most people give up when things start falling apart. People who stay in faith are people who overcome and get rewarded. Once again, I have to repeat the following because understanding it is so crucial: It is not happening *to* you but *from* you and most importantly it's happening *for* you. It's happening for your benefit. When you grasp that idea, you will be able to understand why you get broken, why there are hardships in life. So you can be promoted. That's why. It's just a test. If that person did not leave you, you would never have found the right person for you. If Mark Cuban did not get fired from his job, he might still be doing it for a minimum wage.

8. Discipline

Without discipline, everything falls apart. There has to be consistency. And sometimes it is so hard to resist the temptation of instant gratification and work unnoticed until we reach our final goal. Average people move one little thing and they wait until someone sees it and gives them validation. Successful people keep moving and working while no one is looking. The rest work only when they are being monitored. Your discipline is displayed through your exccllcncc—excellence in your work, in your relationships, in every area in your life.

7. Thoughts

You need to shift your thoughts. You have to possess your thoughts. Whatever you think about on a daily basis has a tendency to manifest one way or another. So you want to get what you *want*, not what are you *fear*. Whatever is your dominant thought, you are stamping it into your mind and communicating with the Universe to give it birth. Your thoughts become distorted by your surroundings and everybody is fighting to take a piece of it. You pay to whatever you focus your attention on. You pay with your time and with your money. After you shift your habits and associations, control of your thoughts might be just a little easier.

6. Habits

You need to shift your habits. If you are in the habit of having, you will always have. Whatever are your habits, that dictates your life. Change your habits—change your life says the mantra. If you are getting unwanted results, you have to figure out what within you is causing it and reverse that.

5. Associations

You need to shift your associations. People so underestimate the values of their associations. A friend of mine, who used to gamble in a cheap casino, told me like this: "I am in that casino every day, alright? So one day I came in and looked around and thought to myself, what a bunch of losers there are in here. Wait a minute. I am here every day. That means that I am not any better than they are." He turned around and never came back to that place to drink or to gamble.

4. Attention

You have to be more alert, focused, and pay attention. Whatever you give the most attention to, it grows. If you give attention to your lack of money, there it goes. If you give your attention to the fact that you have (some) money, there it goes and grows. Rich people recognize opportunities quickly while others wouldn't see one even if you rubbed it in their nose.

3. Action

You need to take action. You can plan all day and night, you can visualize, but without action, your dream is just a wish. And you also have to know how to prioritize. Average people do easy tasks first. Successful people do important tasks first, even if they are not the easiest ones.

2. Acceptance

Are you willing to pay the price? There is a stiff price for success and that is time. Why stiff? Because time you can never get back. There is no lack of resources or anything on this planet. Everything can be created and re-created except our lives, bodies, and time we spend. But in order to succeed, you need to pay with your time first. Like LL Cool J did, like bill Gates did, like Henry Ford and many others did.

1. Decision

is a first step in anything. But success is carried through commitment. So here is how the circle gets closed. You have to make a decision to commit. Joe and Jane Average always ask others what they think and what would they do. Successful people make their own decisions. They make them fast and rarely change them.

HOW TO GET MONEY

HOW TO GET MONEY

THE MASTER KEY TO SUCCESS & WEALTH

by David Jambrovic

Dedication

With love I dedicate this book to my better half, my soulmate, my loving and beautiful wife Valerie